SCORPIO
WITCH
♏

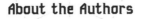

©JAMES C. WELCH

Ivo Dominguez, Jr. (Georgetown, DE) has been active in the magickal community since 1978. He is one of the founders of Keepers of the Holly Chalice, the first Assembly of the Sacred Wheel coven. He currently serves as one of the Elders in the Assembly. Ivo is the author of several books, including *The Four Elements of the Wise* and *Practical Astrology for Witches and Pagans*. In his mundane life, he has been a computer programmer, the executive director of an AIDS/HIV service organization, a bookstore owner, and many other things. Visit him at www.ivodominguezjr.com.

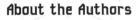

About the Authors

© MICHAEL J. WHITE

Zoë Howe is an internationally published writer, artist, and witch (with her Sun and four planets in Scorpio). She is the author of *Witchful Thinking: The Wise Woman's Handbook for Creating a Charmed Life* (Llewellyn Worldwide, 2022), as well as an array of music books, including her bestselling biography of rock's own witchy woman Stevie Nicks (*Visions, Dreams & Rumours*). A regular host on award-winning UK station Soho Radio with her popular show *The Rock 'n' Roll Witch*, Zoë is a Royal Literary Fund Writing Fellow, and she has appeared on UK TV and radio outlets including the BBC and Sky Arts. Her work has been acclaimed by publications including *The Guardian*, *The Sunday Express*, *Teen Vogue*, *Rolling Stone*, and elsewhere. Zoë is an initiate of Gardnerian Wicca and a member of OBOD.

• UNLOCK THE MAGIC OF YOUR SUN SIGN •

SCORPIO
WITCH

♏

IVO DOMINGUEZ, JR.
ZOË HOWE

Llewellyn Publications
Woodbury, Minnesota

FIRST EDITION
First Printing, 2024

Art direction and cover design by Shira Atakpu
Book design by Christine Ha
Interior art by the Llewellyn Art Department
Tarot Original 1909 Deck © 2021 with art created by Pamela Colman Smith and Arthur Edward Waite. Used with permission of LoScarabeo.
The Scorpio Correspondences appendix is excerpted with permission from *Llewellyn's Complete Book of Correspondences: A Comprehensive & Cross-Referenced Resource for Pagans & Wiccans* © 2013 by Sandra Kynes.

Llewellyn Publications is a registered trademark of Llewellyn Worldwide Ltd.

Library of Congress Cataloging-in-Publication Data
Names: Domínguez, Ivo, Jr., author. | Howe, Zoë, author.
Title: Scorpio witch : unlock the magic of your sun sign : summoning the deep mysteries / Ivo Dominguez, Jr. and Zoë Howe.
Description: First edition. | Woodbury, MN : Llewellyn Publications, [2024] | Series: Witch's sun sign series ; 8
Identifiers: LCCN 2023048920 (print) | LCCN 2023048921 (ebook) | ISBN 9780738772875 (hardcover) | ISBN 9780738772950 (ebook)
Subjects: LCSH: Scorpio (Astrology) | Witchcraft. | Magic.
Classification: LCC BF1727.5 .D66 2024 (print) | LCC BF1727.5 (ebook) | DDC 133.5/273—dc23/eng/20231219
LC record available at https://lccn.loc.gov/2023048920
LC ebook record available at https://lccn.loc.gov/2023048921

Llewellyn Publications
A Division of Llewellyn Worldwide Ltd.
2143 Wooddale Drive
Woodbury, MN 55125-2989
www.llewellyn.com
Printed in the United States of America

Other Books by Ivo Dominguez, Jr.

The Four Elements of the Wise

Keys to Perception: A Practical Guide to Psychic Development

Practical Astrology for Witches and Pagans

Casting Sacred Space

Spirit Speak

Other Books by Zoë Howe

*Witchful Thinking: The Wise Woman's Handbook
to Creating a Charmed Life*

Stevie Nicks: Visions, Dreams & Rumours

Typical Girls? The Story of the Slits

Dayglo: The Poly Styrene Story

Florence + The Machine: An Almighty Sound

Other Books in The Witch's Sun Sign Series

Aries Witch

Taurus Witch

Gemini Witch

Cancer Witch

Leo Witch

Virgo Witch

Libra Witch

Sagittarius Witch

Capricorn Witch

Aquarius Witch

Pisces Witch

CONTENTS

SPELLS, RECIPES, AND PRACTICES

INTRODUCTION

Ivo Dominguez, Jr.

T his is the eighth book in the Witch's Sun Sign series. There are twelve volumes in this series with a book for every Sun sign, but with a special focus on witchcraft. This series explores and honors the gifts, perspectives, and joys of being a witch through the perspective of their Sun sign. Each book has information on how your sign affects your magick and life experiences with insights provided by witches of your Sun sign, as well as spells, rituals, and practices to enrich your witchcraft. This series is geared toward helping witches grow, develop, and integrate the power of their Sun sign into all their practices. Each book in the series has ten writers, so there are many takes on the meaning of being a witch of a particular sign. All the books in the Witch's Sun Sign series are a sampler of possibilities, with pieces that are deep, fun, practical, healing, instructive, revealing, and authentic.

Welcome to the Scorpio Witch

I'm Ivo Dominguez, Jr., and I've been a witch and an astrologer for over forty years. In this book, and in the whole series, I've written the chapters focused on astrological information and collaborated with the other writers. For the sake of transparency, I am a Sagittarius, and the nine other writers for this book are Scorpios. The chapters focused on the lived experience of being a Scorpio witch were written by my coauthor, Zoë Howe. She is an author, a witch, a broadcaster, a visual artist, and a drummer. Zoë has written several books, including *Witchful Thinking: The Wise Woman's Handbook to Creating a Charmed Life* and *Stevie Nicks: Visions, Dreams and Rumours*. She is the embodiment of a rock 'n' roll witch. The spells and shorter pieces written for this book come from a diverse group of strong Scorpio witches. Their practices will give you a deeper understanding of yourself as a Scorpio and as a witch. With the information, insights, and methods offered here, your Scorpio nature and your witchcraft will be better united. The work of becoming fully yourself entails finding, refining, and merging all the parts that make up your life and identity. This all sounds very serious, but the content of this book will run from lighthearted to profound to do justice to the topic. Moreover, this book has practical suggestions on using the power of your Sun sign to improve your craft as a witch. There are many books on Scorpio or astrology or witchcraft; this book is about wholeheartedly being a Scorpio witch.

There is a vast amount of material available in books, blogs, memes, and videos targeted at Scorpio. The content presented in these ranges from serious to snarky and a fair amount of it is less than accurate or useful. After reading this book, you will be better equipped to tell which of these you can take to heart and use, and which are fine for a laugh but not much more. There is a good chance that you will be flipping back to reread some chapters to get a better understanding of some of the points being made. This book is meant to be read more than once, and some parts of it may become reference material that you will use for years. Consider keeping a folder, digital or paper, for your notes and ideas on being a Scorpio witch.

What You Will Need

Knowing your Sun sign is enough to get quite a bit out of this book. However, to use all the material in this book, you will need your birth chart to verify your Moon sign and rising sign. In addition to your birth date, you will need the location and the time of your birth as exactly as possible. If you don't know your birth time, try to get a copy of your birth certificate, though not all birth certificates list times. If it is reasonable and you feel comfortable, you can ask family members for information. They may remember an exact time, but even narrowing it down to a range of hours will be useful. There is a solution to not having your exact birth time. Since it takes moments to create birth charts using software, you can run birth charts that are thirty minutes apart over the span of hours that contains your possible birth times. By reading the chapters that describe the characteristics of Moon signs and rising signs, you can reduce the pile of possible charts to a few contenders. Read the descriptions and find the chart whose combination of Moon sign and rising sign rings true to you. There are more refined techniques that a professional astrologer can use to get closer to a chart that is more accurate. However, knowing your Sun sign, Moon sign, and rising sign is all you need for this book. There are numerous websites that offer free basic birth charts that you can view online. For a fee, more detailed charts are available on these sites.

You may want to have an astrological wall calendar or an astrological day planner. To begin, this may be for keeping track of the sign and phase of the Moon. You will want to keep track of what your ruling planet, the Moon, is doing. Over time as your knowledge grows, you'll probably start looking at where all the planets are, what aspects they are making, and when they are retrograde or direct. You could do this all on an app or at a website, but it is often easier to flip through a calendar or planner to see what is going on than entering and selecting a date at a time. Flipping forward and back through the weeks and months can give you a better sense of how to prepare for upcoming celestial influences. Moreover, the calendars and planner contain basic background information about astrology and are a great start for studying astrology.

You're a Scorpio and So Much More

Every person is unique, complex, and a mixture of traits that can clash, complement, compete, or collaborate with each other. This book focuses on your Scorpio Sun sign and provides starting points for understanding your Moon sign and rising sign. It cannot answer all your questions or be a perfect fit because of all the other parts that make you an individual. However, you will find more than enough to enrich and deepen your witchcraft as a Scorpio. There will also be descriptions that you won't agree with or that you think do not portray you. In some instances, you will be correct, and in other cases you may come around to acknowledging that the information does apply to you. Astrology can be used for magick, divination, personal development, and more. No matter the purpose, your understanding of astrology will change over time as your life unfolds and your experience and self-knowledge broaden. You will probably return to this book several times as you find opportunities to use more of the insights and methods.

This may seem like strange advice to find in a book for the Scorpio witch, but remember that you are more than a Scorpio witch. In the process of claiming the identity of being a witch, it is common to want to have a clear and firm definition of who you are. Sometimes this means overidentifying with a category, such as water witch, herb witch, crystal witch, kitchen witch, and so on. It is useful to become aware of the affinities that you have so long as you do not limit and bind yourself to being less than you are. The best use for this book is to uncover all the parts of you that are Scorpio so you can integrate them well. The finest witches I know have well-developed specialties but also are well rounded in their knowledge and practices.

Onward!

With all that said, the Sun is the starting point for your power and your journey as a witch. The first chapter is about the profound influence your Sun sign has, so don't skip through the table of contents; please start at the beginning. After that, Zoë will dive into magick and practices that come naturally to Scorpio witches. I'll be walking you through the benefits of picking the right times, places, and things to energize your Scorpio magick. Zoë will also share a couple of real-life personal stories on her ups and downs, as well as advice on the best ways to protect yourself spiritually and set good boundaries when you really need to. I'll introduce you to how your Moon sign and your rising sign shape your witchcraft. Zoë offers great stories about how her Scorpio nature comes forward in her life as a witch, and then gives suggestions on self-care and self-awareness. I'll share a full ritual with you to call on the spirit of your sign. Lastly, Zoë offers her wisdom on how to become a better Scorpio witch. Throughout the whole book, you'll find tables of correspondences, spells, recipes, techniques, and other treasures to add to your practices.

HOW YOUR SUN
POWERS YOUR MAGICK

Ivo Dominguez, Jr.

The first bit of astrology that people generally learn is their Sun sign. Some enthusiastically embrace the meaning of their Sun sign and apply it to everything in their life. They feel their Sun is shining and all is well in the world. Then at some point they'll encounter someone who will, with a bit of disdain, enlighten them on the limits of Sun sign astrology. They feel their Sun isn't enough and they scramble to catch up. What comes next is usually the discovery that they have a Moon sign, a rising sign, and all the rest of the planets in an assortment of signs. Making sense of all this additional information is daunting as it requires quite a bit of learning and/or an astrologer to guide you through the process. Wherever you are in this or similar journeys into the world of astrology, at some point you will circle back around and rediscover that the Sun is still in the center.

The Sun in your birth chart shows where life and spirit came into the world to form you. It is the keeper of your spark of spirit and the wellspring of your power. Your Sun is in Scorpio, so that is the flavor, the color, the type of energy that is at your core. You are your whole birth chart, but it is your Scorpio Sun that provides the vital force that moves throughout all parts of your life. When you work in harmony and alignment with your Sun, you have access to more life and the capacity to live it better. This is true for all people, but this advice takes on a special meaning for those who are witches. The root of a witch's magick power is revealed by their Sun sign. You can draw on many kinds of energy, but the type of energy that you attract with greatest ease is Scorpio. The more awareness and intention you apply to connecting with and acting as a conduit for that Scorpio Sun, the more effective you will be as a witch.

The more you learn about the meaning of a Scorpio Sun, the easier it will be to find ways to make that connection. To be effective in magick, divination, and other categories of workings, it is vital that you understand yourself, your motivations, drives, attractions, and so on so that you can refine your intentions, questions, and desired outcomes. Understanding your Scorpio sign is an important step in that process. One of the goals shared by both witchcraft and astrology is to affirm and to integrate the totality of your nature to live your best life. The glyph for the Sun in astrology is a dot

with a circle around it. Your Scorpio Sun is the dot
and the circle, your center, and your circumference.
It is your beginning and your journey. It is also
the core of your personal Wheel of the Year—the seasons of
your life that repeat, have resonances, but are never the same.

How Scorpio Are You?

The Sun is the hub around which the planets circle. Its gravity pulls the planets to keep them in their courses and bends
space-time to create the place we call our solar system. The
Sun in your birth chart tugs on every other part of your chart
in a similar way. Everything is both bound and free, affected
but seeking its own direction. When people encounter
descriptions of Scorpio traits, they will often begin to make
a list of which things apply to them and which don't. Some
will say that they are the epitome of Scorpio traits, others
will claim that they are barely Scorpio, and many will be
somewhere in between. Evaluating how closely or not you
align with the traditional characteristics of a Scorpio is not
a particularly useful approach to understanding your sign. If
you are a Scorpio, you have all the Scorpio traits somewhere
within you. What varies from person to person is the expression of those traits. Some traits express fully in a classic form,
others are blocked from expressing, or are modified, and
sometimes there is a reaction to behave as the opposite of
what is expected. As a Scorpio, and especially as a witch, you

have the capacity to activate dormant traits, to shape functioning traits, and to tone down overactive traits.

The characteristics and traits of signs are tendencies, drives, and affinities. Gravity encourages a ball to roll down a hill. A plant's leaves will grow in the direction of sunlight. The warmth of a fire will draw people together on a cold night. A flavor that you enjoy will entice you to take another bite of your food. Your Scorpio Sun urges you to be and to act like a Scorpio. That said, you also have free will and volition to make other choices. Moreover, the rest of your birth chart and the ever-changing celestial influences are also shaping your options, moods, and drives. The more you become aware of the traits and behaviors that come with being a Scorpio, the easier it will be to choose how you express them. Most people want to have the freedom to explore themselves and make a difference in the world, but for a Scorpio, it is essential for their well-being.

As a witch, you have additional tools to work with the Scorpio energy. You can choose when to access and how you shape the qualities of Scorpio as they come forth in your life. You can summon the energy of Scorpio, name the traits you desire, and manifest them. You can also banish or neutralize or ground what you don't need. You can find where your Scorpio energy short-circuits, where it glitches, and unblock it. You can examine your uncomfortable feelings and your less-than-perfect behaviors to seek the shadowed places within so you can heal or integrate them. Scorpio is a spirit and a current of collective consciousness that is vast in size. Scorpio is also a group mind and archetype. Scorpio is not limited to humanity; it engages with plants, animals, minerals, and all the physical and nonphysical beings of the Earth and all its associated realms. As a witch, you can call upon and work with the spiritual entity that is Scorpio. You can live your life as a ritual. The motion of your life can be a dance to the tune and rhythm of the heavens.

The Scorpio Glyph

The glyph for Scorpio looks a bit like the glyph for Virgo because they both contain a shape that resembles the letter *m*. Scorpio's glyph has an arrowlike stinger as opposed to the crossed curve of Virgo.
In the pictographic code of the astrological glyphs, vertical lines connect the above and the below; circles, loops, and semicircles represent spirit and soul. Spirit is the part of you that is eternal, and soul is the part that is shaped and changed by the experiences of incarnation. The glyph for Scorpio tells the story of a journey back and forth between the heights and the depths with a sharp arrow that cuts through to reveal the heart of things. The glyph speaks of the need to remember that life is a series of cycles and that your path is about mastering the twists and turns. This work is about making the

unknown visible and embracing and integrating all the parts of your being.

With the use of your imagination, you can see this glyph as a scorpion or a sidewinding serpent. The shape of the glyph can be interpreted as waves of power spreading outward and pushing the cutting edge forward. It is an echo of the glyphs for Mars and Pluto. The glyph is also the secret rites of union and merging that are the hidden teachings of sexuality. It is Scorpio's job to dig deeper and to not look away until all that can be understood is absorbed. The closer you look at the glyph and contemplate it, the more you see. Scorpio's gift is to embrace life in all its forms and possibilities.

By meditating on the glyph, you will develop a deeper understanding of what it is to be a Scorpio. You may also come up with your own personal myth or story about the glyph that can be a key that is uniquely yours. The glyph for Scorpio can be used as a sigil to call or concentrate its power. The glyph for Scorpio can be used in a similar fashion to the scribing of an invoking pentacle that is used to open the gates to the elemental realms. However, instead of the elemental realms, this glyph opens the way to the realm of emotions and mystical knowledge that is the source of Scorpio. To make this glyph work, you need to deeply ingrain the feeling of scribing this glyph. Visually, it is a simple glyph, so memorizing it is easy, but having a kinesthetic feel for it turns it into magick. Spend some time doodling the glyph on paper. Try drawing the glyph on your palm with a finger for several repetitions as that adds several layers of sensation and memory patterns.

Whenever you need access to more of your magickal energy, scribe the Scorpio glyph in your mind, on your hand, in the air, however you can. Then pull, channel, and feel your center fill with whatever you need. It takes very little time to open this connection using the glyph. Consider making this one of the practices you use to get ready to do divination, spell work, ritual, or just to start your day.

Scorpio Patterns

This is a short list of patterns, guidelines, and predilections for Scorpio Sun people to get you started. If you keep a book of shadows, or a journal, or files on a digital device to record your thoughts and insights on magickal work, you may wish to create your own list to expand upon these. The process of observing, summarizing, and writing down your own ideas in a list is a great way to learn about your sign.

- Although a water sign, Scorpio is often described as fiery. This may come from people confusing and conflating spiciness, passion, and emotional intensity with fire. Ice can feel like fire as well.

- Scorpio doesn't want to look away until they see the raw truth, the essence, of a person, a situation, or the matters of the world.

- The more something is obscured, tucked away, kept locked up, or secret, the more a Scorpio will do whatever is needed to examine it.

- You need intimacy and deep connections with the people who are dear to you as much as you need to breathe. You are likely to regularly test the people in your life.

- You tend to be secretive at the same time that you give the impression of showing who you are. Having taken a profound look into human nature, you may doubt that others will want to see your whole truth.

- Scorpios are called to walk straight into the mysteries of sex, death, loss, and regeneration. Sometimes you are the moth and sometimes you are the flame.

- When you are wronged or threatened, you have a powerful sting whose venom can be as dangerous to you as it is to others. Seeking justice is not revenge or a witty clapback.

- Three of the most common symbols for Scorpio are the scorpion, the eagle, and the phoenix. These are the emblems of your lower, middle, and higher Self. The goal is to be all three at once.

A healthy Scorpio learns to feel things fully and then to release them. This does not mean forgetting; it means remembering and integrating the lesson. This creates emotional muscle and resiliency instead of scar tissue and restrictions in your spirit.

Your gaze has power because you look into the windows of the soul that eyes provide. Try to let others look into your eyes as well.

You know at a gut level when others need your compassion. It is not always your job to intervene, but the sincerity of your presence is often enough to be helpful.

The world is complicated enough as it is; aim for clarity and simplicity when you are trying to extract meaning from your experiences.

You can handle almost anything and recover from it. In fact, you can come back stronger. Be mindful that you can escalate things faster than you can manage, so learn to pace yourself.

- You regularly and routinely have feelings that are deeper and vaster than many people can cope with. When you find people who can handle you, hang on to them. The challenge may be to find the balance between being protective or being possessive of those stout souls.

- If things get out of hand, you may feel that the world is out to get you. You do see more sharply than most, but none of us sees the whole picture. Awaken your humor and summon your courage; you'll find the way through and out of perils both real and imagined.

- Most Scorpios have great personal magnetism and radiate a power that can attract, fascinate, or frighten people. Try to remain aware of this power and use it with conscious intent.

- When you take care of yourself, you have great stamina, competitive drive, and can be a workaholic. There is little that can stop you when you have a goal in mind.

Scorpios become laser-focused on whatever interests them. This is a useful ability, but you can become hyper-focused and get tunnel vision. This can lead to problems and is one of the reasons why it can be hard for you to change your course or decisions. Try to let go of the focus and look around to see what else is affecting your circumstances.

You tend to be fascinated by the darker side of things, spooky occurrences, the other realms of reality, and things that go bump in the night even more than most witches of any sign.

Most Scorpios have an undercurrent of thoughts and feelings related to sexuality, sensuality, and emotional connection running under the flow of their main stream of thought.

Fixed Water

The four elements come in sets of three. The modalities known as cardinal, fixed, and mutable are three different flavors or styles of manifestation for the elements. The twelvefold pattern that is the backbone of astrology comes from the twelve combinations produced from four elements times three modalities. As you go around the wheel  of the zodiac, the order of the elements is always fire, earth, air, then water, while the modalities are always in the order of cardinal, fixed, then mutable. Each season begins in the cardinal modality, reaches its peak in the fixed modality, and transforms to the next season in the mutable modality. The cardinal modality is the energy of creation bursting forth, coming into being, and spreading throughout the world. The fixed modality is the harmonization of energy so that it becomes and remains fully itself and is preserved. The mutable modality is the energy of flux that is flexibility, transformation, death, and rebirth.

Scorpio is the eighth sign in the zodiac, so it is water of the fixed modality. This is why a Scorpio witch can call up power to interrogate reality so passionately. As a Scorpio witch, you can call upon water in all its forms; it is easiest to draw upon fixed water.

The elements and modalities on the wheel

Pluto, Your Ruling Planet

Your Sun sign determines the source and the type of energy that you have in your core. The ruling planet for a sign reveals your go-to moves and your intuitive or habitual responses for expressing that energy. Your ruling planet provides a curated set of prebuilt responses and custom-tailored stances for you to use in day-to-day life. Mars was the planet that was originally assigned to Scorpio. In modern times, Pluto became assigned as its primary ruler. The name of this planet may bring to mind the Greek Hades or the Roman Pluto, the sovereigns of the underworld in their pantheons. However, the planet Pluto and how it influences Scorpio is about more than a connection to the underworld. All the hidden places within the mind, heart, and spirit are also Pluto's domain. Since Scorpio is a water sign, this encourages the expression of Pluto to take focus on emotions, passions, and transformation. All deities related to sexuality, death, rebirth, magick, and so on link to Scorpio through this watery Pluto. The touch of Hecate, Freya, Osiris is here as well as many others. Pluto's glyph suggests a bident or stang with a sphere of energy suspended between the tines. Scorpio likes to wield this to bring about the magick of transformation, which when seen as a whole is the stillness of eternity.

Scorpio witches are more strongly affected by whatever Pluto is doing in the heavens, and to a lesser degree Mars. It is useful to keep track of the aspects that Pluto is making with other planets. You can get basic information on what aspects mean and when they are happening in astrological calendars and online resources. You will feel Pluto retrogrades more strongly than most people, but you can find ways to make them useful periods to integrate what you have already experienced. Pluto moves slowly through the heavens, so it won't be back in Scorpio during your lifetime. However, when Mars in the heavens makes aspects to Pluto, you will feel your magick change in response to the nature of that aspect. You will also have a boost of power when the Sun is in the same degree as Pluto in your birth chart. Witches can shift their relationship with the powers that influence them. Your awareness of these powers makes it possible to harness those energies to purposes that you choose. Close your eyes, feel for that power, and channel it into your magick.

Pluto can be as great a source of energy for a Scorpio witch as the element of water. Although there is some overlap between the qualities and capacities assigned to Pluto and water, the differences are greater. Pluto pushes you to change and transform, to die and be reborn. Water is the medium of life that is both the waters of birth and of dissolution. Pluto rules the forces that are so vast they cannot be overcome. Water seeks the lowest point and takes on the shape and motion of all it encounters. Pluto has an agenda to bring about a testing that either sponsors evolution or brings about the extinction of what is no longer viable. Water nurtures growth, wears away the sharp edges, and eventually yields life after turning rot into fertile compost. Water is the principle of healing through cycles of the heart and contains the spirit of resilience. Water is the surface that can reflect to bring forth wisdom. Over time you can map out the overlapping regions and the differences between Pluto and water. Using both planetary and elemental resources can give you a much broader range and more finesse.

Scorpio and the Zodiacal Wheel

The order of the signs in the zodiac can also be seen as a creation story where the run of the elements repeats three times. Scorpio is in the second third of the zodiac and ends the second run of the four elements in the story of the universe. Having come into existence, the goal of the elements at this point of the story is to become fully themselves. The water of Scorpio tries to understand itself, how it connects with others, and what it will be next. It evaluates what is within so that it might come to embrace their place in the unfolding story of personal and collective existence. Although Scorpio is often stereotyped as too prone to strong emotional actions and strong judgments, the deeper truth is that they know what is at stake when authenticity and integrity are lost. Although true for all witches, the Scorpio witch needs to accept themselves and see themselves as works in progress. When you can consistently connect with your Scorpio nature that is your core self, you become the power that can heal and restore anything. You can make progress in this quest through meditation and inner journeys, but that alone will not do. The Scorpio witch learns by doing inner work and then applying their insights in the world. When a Scorpio witch connects to the spiritual qualities of water, they become the counselor whose words and actions encourage a blessed state of peace within and without.

The sign and planet rulers on the zodiac wheel

SCORPIO
CORRESPONDENCES

♏

Power: To Desire

Keyword: Regeneration

Roles: Catalyst, Investigator, Facilitator

Ruling Planets: Pluto with Mars ♇ as a secondary ruler

Element: Fixed Water

Colors: Crimson, Black, Dark Purple, Dark Shades

Shapes: Pentagon and Nonagon

Metal: Steel

Body Parts Ruled: Sexual Organs

Day of the Week: Tuesday

Affirmation:
*I will live authentically, and
I will live in my whole truth.*

WITCHCRAFT THAT COMES NATURALLY TO A SCORPIO

Zoë Howe

Scorpio Season IS the season of the witch—it encompasses Samhain, All Souls', the Night of Hecate (November 16) and the shift into darkness—and Scorpio as a sign is about power, control and transformation, manipulation and focus, the psyche and its shadows. It's no surprise, therefore, that Scorpios are considered naturals when it comes to magical practice. It's also no surprise that we seem to strike fear into the hearts of many, or indeed that Scorpio is the most misunderstood sign of the zodiac. Witches across time are, of course, quite used to facing down these often distorted preconceptions, so for the Scorpio witch, this is nothing unusual.

Us Hallowe'en babies are dedicated, intuitive, leftfield, analytical, and perceptive—the Sherlock Holmes of the cosmos, in all of his eccentric, remote, and rebellious glory. We also feel intensely, often to extremes. This can sound like a bad thing, but when we focus our emotions and channel them into our magical work, we achieve significant results.

Thanks to these qualities, not to mention a natural tendency toward obsession and an often tunnel-visioned approach to our goals, we excel at occult work, divination, intuiting people's motives, and analyzing our dreams. That's not to say other signs don't excel at those things, but Scorpio may find they are simply second nature—you might have grown up thinking that surely *everyone* must be busy bending reality, so normal is it for the typical Scorp. From sex magic to shadow work, Scorpio dives in and goes deep, lifting the stone to see what's crawling around in the dark, sashaying forth where others fear to tread.

You probably don't mind people knowing you're a witch—in fact you'd be disappointed if they didn't just assume it, with all those waves of power emanating from you. You're less likely than other signs to "proclaim" it—you don't need to—but those who work it out for themselves will probably be friends for life, if you let your guard down. Independent Scorpio can often be found working happily solitaire; we like to do things our way, usually in private. We like to write or tailor our own, often no-frills, spells and rituals rather than use other people's; there is little patience for one-size-fits-all spellcraft here.

We are not followers, but we might not be leaders either—we flow with our own energy and go where it directs us, using our "magic" words, laser focus, and sheer will; we know the power comes from within us. Scorpio pares things back to the bone, the essence; we like to clear everything aside and see the truth, and this connects with the kind of magic and energy work we do. Never mind the fripperies and fancy stuff—a simple but intense meditation or a written intention is often all we need to effect change.

Spiritual Healing and Spirit Connections

Healing comes naturally to Scorpio, whether hands-on or distant, and techniques that involve us uniting mind, body, and spirit in service are where we can use our considerable power for good. My Scorpio grandfather, now in Spirit, was a quietly powerful healer himself, and his down-to-Earth demeanor and cheeky humor belied a deeply spiritual side. I can sense him drawing close as I write this, proudly wearing his Mars-red sweater and exclaiming "Scorpios unite!" as we always used to do. This brings us neatly onto the subject of spiritual connection.

Communication with Spirit and the divine, whether through meditative conversations or sincere, respectful petitions, can bring beautiful results and make us feel held; for lone-wolf Scorp, this is a moving experience. In touch with our inner hermit, we may be satisfied as a solitary practitioner unless a *very* special group presents itself; magical work is sacred and we, the Zodiac's least trusting sign, have to feel certain before we allow ourselves to be vulnerable in the presence of others. We may doubt the intentions of another human, witch or otherwise. But a spirit hug? That loving, tingling rush of energy that confirms the presence of Spirit or the divine? Nothing like it. So while we may *appear* solitary, we know we are always accompanied, and Spirit is often the kind of company we are happiest to keep.

Keep spirit communication respectful, loving, and collaborative—and always be mindful of free will. Never let a sense of power get out of hand. Power is intoxicating, and it's a word often linked with Scorpio, usually in a pejorative sense. But we are as likely to use our power for good, and when we focus on work that blesses others and the planet as well as ourselves, we make a tangible difference.

To Know, to Dare, to Will, and to Keep Silent

This tenet is considered by many to be a vital principle for magical work, but at the same time, it could simply describe a regular Scorpio day. Self-educators to the max, we crave knowledge (often the more arcane the better) and are obsessed with expanding our wisdom. *Daring* is certainly a Scorpio quality, and—depending on the rest of our chart, our conditioning, and the circumstances in which we live—we are often fearless in our natural state. Our will is steely, and as for silence? We are famously secretive. I mean, our ruler is Pluto, enigmatic and remote Lord of the Underworld—keeping silent was never going to be a problem. We know that blabbing dilutes our work and leaves it open to manipulation from external sources. *Paranoid*, us? Well … yes. Although I prefer *wisely cautious*.

The Magical Mindset

Scorpio mind power is such that we may be working magic when we don't even realize it, so it is important to be aware of our words and thoughts. We are inadvertently quite good at compelling, so, again, be aware of respecting others' free will. This is good spiritual hygiene, but also can help us preserve energy and hone how swiftly we are able to manifest, consciously or otherwise. By being deliberate and controlled—rather than letting our gifts control us, or come and go—we can use our focus to harness the powers inherent to us, and this keeps us flowing ever forward in our magical life. Yes, wonderful things will happen unbidden, synchronicities will encourage us, but it is up to us to take the correct steps to acknowledge, welcome, and embrace those synchs and signs, and that means being conscious, deliberate, and committed. This is not difficult for a Scorpio. This is the magical mindset—a mindset that takes magical possibilities into account every moment of every day, finds meaning in the mundane, and knows a message when it perceives one.

We are tough and brave, but flexibility is also key because we must always expect the unexpected and have an inkling of what to do when we meet it. However, our sense of permanence can be such that, once we've manifested a result, if it's not what we'd hoped for, we might feel we have to commit anyway and stoically make the best of it. But if you have the knowledge, power, and will to manifest something, you have the skills to unmanifest it. Take care with your wording and thoughts and the energy within and around the situation; lack of due care in that respect may be why the result wasn't what you'd hoped for in the first place.

Scorpios aren't known as the most flexible of signs, but keep in mind an image of the scorpion itself and its physicality if you need reminding of what our counterpart critter is capable of: it has an exoskeleton made up of plates and segments, and it can move and arch and even dance (yes, when courting, they can dance a sweet *pas de deux* for up to an hour). Inflexible? I think not. Stay adaptable, Scorpio witch. We might be the control freaks of the heavens, but we always find a way if we allow ourselves to try—and if we don't get bogged down with regret over getting it "wrong" the first time. We can handle anything. We might not trust ourselves to, but we can.

Simple Elemental Workings

Scorpio shares the water element with Pisces and Cancer, but, as Ivo has observed, people often associate Scorpio with fire, being as we are more ferocious than our elemental brethren. We can certainly burn through blocks and obstacles when we invoke the fire of Scorpio archetype, the phoenix, and the scorpion also represents the one water sign that resides on land. If we were to read meaning into that—and Scorpios always will—we might interpret this as an extra boon, grounding us and minimizing watery illusions misting up our view. But it could also explain why we sometimes need a little help going with the flow.

If you compare us to the fire signs, there are differences in how we express our heat—again, as Ivo noted earlier, our "fire" is more like ice, as anyone who has been "frozen out" by a scorned Scorp will know. Fire can swiftly and irreversibly transform, but water's hypnotic power has the ability to fool you, and it can quickly overwhelm and destroy. It is not to be underestimated.

Our fire sign friends rage and roar, but we are more likely to go terrifyingly silent, leaving our enemies wondering what on Earth we're going to do—and when. Cue evil laugh and a swish of a cape—or rather the swish of a sting, lashing at its target with devastating precision. Are we as bad as we're painted? Once I would have reassuringly protested, "No! We're just misunderstood." Now I'm older and more at home with my sting, and so I say, "Yes ... when we need to be. So be careful."

As ever, depending on the rest of your chart, you may find yourself preferring to work with a different element. That said, as humans we contain all the elements, and as witches we honor them all, not just one. Here are some simple, natural ideas for you to use or adapt when considering how to connect with the elements:

Water

Divination comes naturally to perceptive Scorpio, and, as water relates to the psychic realms, just peering into water and allowing our gaze to soften into trance can be illuminating when searching for answers or connecting with Spirit. Alternatively, you might want to cast a quick spell that draws on the energy of water but has a more active nature. Take a piece of paper, some water-soluble ink, and a glass of rainwater, preferably collected during a waning Moon (for decrease). Write down something you want to rid yourself of—you could use the Abracadabra Spell for this (page 212) if you wish. Once you have written on the paper, hold it in your hands, charging it with your intention, and then drop it into the water—the ink will quickly dissolve. Remove the paper and flush the water down the toilet immediately, or dispose of it in a flowing waterway away from your home.

Fire

Tap into the energy of Samhain; not only is it a key fire festival, it is *our* fire festival, falling as it does in Scorpio season. Gather some leaves from the ground if it is fall and write your wishes onto them. Light a fire if it is safe for you to do so (use a steel saucepan outside on a still night if you don't have a fireplace) and intentionally cast the leaves into the fire or set them alight, imagining the situations transforming as the leaves change state. (If it is not fall, don't pull leaves off the tree to do this—it's fine to use paper!)

Air

There's something special about the sound of a bell to start and conclude a ritual, and when you consider how sound works, the striking of metal against metal and the resounding chime has magical significance—the chime gradually reducing in audibility into apparent nothingness. We can use this idea to inspire us, reflective as it is of our intention in the material world going out into the invisible realm, reverberating even as we lose our own perception of it. Make a wish and peal the bell. As the sound softens, know your intention is traveling to where it needs to be.

Earth

Write a charm, intention, or message to Spirit on a leaf, or etch it with a toothpick into a piece of fruit and bury it in the ground. As it inevitably breaks down, nourishing the earth and feeding the bugs and birds, so does the energy change, and your wish in the material world enters that of the unseen. This little spell is very Scorpio in the sense that it connects with the death and transformation energy of Pluto, our coruler with Mars. Scorpio faces the dark stuff with ease and curiosity, and so this kind of entropy magic is perfectly simpatico.

MAGICAL
CORRESPONDENCES
Zoë Howe

As a Scorpio, you'll find that certain kinds of spells, tools, and workings suit your particular nature more than others. Here are some thoughts about the kind of magic Scorpio connects with, herbs and tools that align with your energy, and ideas to weave into your magical practice, if you wish.

Types of Spellcraft

+ Ritual baths
+ Blood magic
+ Sex magic
+ Dark Moon work
+ Freezer spells
+ Water scrying
+ Dream analysis

Magical Tools

- Colors: red, black, burgundy
- Baneful herbs
- Black crystals
- Metals—especially iron
- Essential oils of benzoin, black pepper, clove, and frankincense
- Black salt
- Boxes for secrets!
- Will, focus, and determination

Magical Goals and Spell Ideas

- Working with the day (Tuesday) and planetary hour of Mars
- Psychic protection
- Healing
- Using visualization, meditation, and self-hypnosis
- Banishing and boundary magic
- Empowerment spells
- Working with past lives to heal the present

Ivo Dominguez, Jr.

You've probably encountered plenty of charts and lists in books and online, cataloging which things relate to your Sun sign and ruling planet. There are many gorgeously curated assortments of herbs, crystals, music playlists, fashions, sports, fictional characters, tarot cards, and more that are assigned to your Sun sign. These compilations of associations are more than a curiosity or for entertainment. Correspondences are like treasure maps to show you where to find the type and flavor of power you are seeking. Correspondences are flowcharts and diagrams that show the inner occult relationship between subtle energies and the physical world. Although there are many purposes for lists of correspondences, there are two that are especially valuable to becoming a better Scorpio witch.

The first is to contemplate the meaning of the correspondences, the ways in which they reveal meaningful details about your Sun sign and ruling planet, and how they connect to you. This will deepen your understanding of what it is to be a Scorpio witch. The second is to use these items as points of connection to access energies and essences that support your witchcraft. This will expand the number of tools and resources at your disposal for all your efforts.

Each of the sections in this chapter will introduce you to a type of correlation with suggestions on how to identify and use it. These are just starting points, and you will find many more as you explore and learn. As you broaden your knowledge, you may find yourself a little bit confused as you find that sources disagree on the correlations. These contradictions are generally not a matter of who is in error but a matter of perspective, cultural differences, and the intended uses for the correlations. Anything that exists in the physical world can be described as a mixture of all the elements, planets, and signs. You may be a Scorpio, but depending on the rest of your chart, there may be strong concentrations of other signs and elements. For example, if you find that a particular herb is listed as associated with both Scorpio and Aries, it is because it contains both natures in abundance. In the cases of strong multiple correlations, it is important to summon or tune in to the one you need.

Times

You always have access to your power as a Scorpio witch, but there are times when the flow is stronger, readily available, or more easily summoned. There are sophisticated astrological methods to select dates and times that are specific to your birth chart. Unless you want to learn quite a bit more astrology or hire someone to determine these for you, you can do quite well with simpler methods. Let's look at the cycles of the solar year, the lunar month, and the hours of day-night rotation. When the Sun is in Scorpio, or the Moon is in Scorpio, or it is the beginning of the night, you are in the sweet spot for tuning in to the core of your power.

Scorpio season is roughly October 23– November 21, but check your astrological calendar or ephemeris to determine when it is for a specific year in your time zone. The amount of accessible energy is highest when the Sun is at the same degree of Scorpio as it is in your birth chart. This peak will not always be on your birth date but very close to it. Midway through Scorpio season is another peak for all Scorpios. Take advantage of Scorpio season for working magick and for recharging and storing up energy for the whole year.

The Moon moves through the twelve signs every lunar cycle and spends around two and half days in each sign. When the Moon is in Scorpio you have access to more lunar power because the Moon in the heavens has a resonant link to the Sun in your birth chart. At some point during its time in Scorpio, the Moon will be at the same degree as your Sun. For you that will be the peak of the energy during the Moon's passage through Scorpio that month. While the Moon is in Scorpio, your psychism is stronger, as is your ability to manifest things. When the Moon is in a waning crescent, in any sign, you can draw upon its power more readily because it is resonant to your sign.

Of the eight holidays in the Wheel of the Year, Scorpio season is Samhain in the northern hemisphere and Beltane in the southern hemisphere. All the fixed signs anchor one of the powerful holidays when they are at their fifteenth degree. The stations of the year, the holidays, are liminal times of transition. The fixed water of Scorpio fills the liminal space of the holiday, making it a cauldron of change. Scorpio is the eighth sign of the zodiac, and the zodiac is like a clock for the purpose of spell work. The first part of true night corresponds to the power of Scorpio. If you are detail focused, you might be wondering when true night begins. This varies with the time of year and with your location, but if you must have a time, think of it as 8:00 p.m. to 10:00 p.m. Or you can use your intuition and feel your way to when true night has begun, when no sunlight remains in the sky. The powers that flow during this time are filled with anticipation, a frisson of fear, and excitement for you to experience. Plan on using the

Scorpio energy of the night for inspiration and to feed spells for learning, divination, empowerment, and change.

The effect of these special times can be joined in any combination. For example, you can choose to do work at the start of night when the Moon is in Scorpio, or the Sun is in Scorpio at the start of night, or the Moon is in Scorpio during Scorpio season. You can combine all three as well. Each of these time period groupings will have a distinctive feeling. Experiment and use your instincts to discover how to use these in your work.

Places

There are activities, professions, phenomena, and behaviors that have an affinity, a resonant connection, to Scorpio and its ruling planet, Pluto. These activities occur in the locations that suit or facilitate their expressions. There is magick to be claimed from those places that is earmarked for Scorpio or your ruling planet, Pluto. Just like your birth chart, the world around you contains the influences of all the planets and signs, but in different proportions and arrangements. You can always draw upon Scorpio or Pluto energy, though there are times when it is more abundant depending on astrological considerations. Places and spaces have energies that accumulate and can be tapped like a battery. Places contain the physical, emotional, and spiritual environments that are created by the actions of the material objects, plants, animals, and people occupying those spaces. Some of the interactions between these things can generate or concentrate the energies and patterns that can be used by Scorpio witches.

If you look at traditional astrology books, you'll find listings of places assigned to Scorpio and Pluto that include locations such as these:

- Caverns, caves, and grottoes
- Graveyards, cemeteries, and morgues
- Places where people are looking for sex
- Dark forests, deep valleys, and places of mystery
- Places of worldly power and wealth, stock markets, boardrooms

These are very clearly linked to the themes associated with Scorpio and Pluto. With a bit of brainstorming and free-associating, you'll find many other less obvious locations and situations where you can draw upon this power. For example, wherever detectives, therapists, social workers, or researchers are at work can produce a current you can plug into. Any situation where you use your intellect or insight to reveal what is hidden or uncomfortable or engage in similar high-focus activities can become a source of Scorpio power. All implements or actions related to risky, daring activities that make your adrenalin spike could also be sources for energy.

While you can certainly go to places that are identified as locations where Scorpio and/or Pluto energy is plentiful to do workings, you can find those energies in many other circumstances. Don't be limited by the idea that the places must be the ones that have a formalized link to Scorpio. Be on the lookout for Scorpio or Pluto themes and activities wherever you may be. Remember that people thinking, feeling, or participating in activities connected to your sign and its ruling planet are raising power. If you can identify with it as resonating with your Sun sign or ruling planet, then you can call the power and put it to use. You complete the circuit to engage the flow with your visualization, intentions, and actions.

Plants

Scorpio is drawn to seeking intensity, altered states of consciousness, and sensuality, and its colors are dark reds, deep violet, and black. Pluto strengthens a connection to the spirit realm, compulsions, and currents of power that stir your depths. Herbs, resins, oils, fruits, vegetables, woods, and flowers that strongly exhibit one or more of these qualities can be called upon to support your magic. Here are a few examples:

- Amaranth speeds physical and emotional regeneration.
- Red geranium to ward and to warn of trouble at your door.
- Black pepper to release negative emotions.
- Acacia to strengthen your will and call courage.
- Patchouli for stirring the passions.

Once you understand the rationale for making these assignments, the lists of correspondences will make more sense. Another thing to consider is that each part of a plant may resonate more strongly with a different element, planet, and sign. Red geranium shows its connection with Scorpio and Pluto with its capacity to regrow from a cutting or revive after being almost dead. However, red geranium is also an herb of Aries and Mars because of its red color, strong scent, and protective energy. Which energy steps forward depends on your call and invitation. *Like calls to like* is a truism in witchcraft. When you use your Scorpio nature to make a call, you are answered by the Scorpio part of the plant.

Plant materials can take the form of incense, anointing oils, altar pieces, potions, washes, magickal implements, foods, flower arrangements, and so on. The mere presence of plant material that is linked to Scorpio or Pluto will be helpful to you. However, to gain the most benefit from plant energy, you need to actively engage with it. Push some of your energy into the plants and then pull on it to start the flow. Although much of the plant material you work with will be dried or preserved, it retains a connection to living members of its species. You may also want to reach out and try to commune with the spirit, the group soul, of the plants to request its assistance or guidance. This will awaken the power slumbering in the dried or preserved plant material. Spending time with living plants, whether they be houseplants, in your yard, or in a public garden, will strengthen your conversation with the green beings under Scorpio's eye.

Crystals and Stones

Before digging into this topic, let's clear up some of the confusion around the birthstones for the signs of the zodiac. There are many varying lists for birthstones. Also be aware that some are related to the calendar month rather than the zodiacal signs. There are traditional lists, but the most commonly available lists for birthstones were created by jewelers to sell more jewelry. Also be cautious of the word *traditional* as some jewelers refer to the older lists compiled by jewelers as "traditional." The traditional lists created by magickal practitioners also diverge from each other because of cultural differences and the availability of different stones in the times and places the lists were created. If you have already formed a strong connection to a birthstone that you discover is not really connected to the energy of your sign, keep using it. Your connection is proof of its value to you in moving, holding, and shifting energy, whether or not it is specifically attuned to Scorpio.

These are my preferred assignments of birthstones for the signs of the zodiac:

Aries	Bloodstone, Carnelian, Diamond
Taurus	Rose Quartz, Amber, Sapphire
Gemini	Agate, Tiger's Eyes, Citrine
Cancer	Moonstone, Pearl, Emerald
Leo	Heliodor, Peridot, Black Onyx
Virgo	Green Aventurine, Moss Agate, Zircon
Libra	Jade, Lapis Lazuli, Labradorite
Scorpio	Obsidian, Pale Beryl, Nuummite
Sagittarius	Turquoise, Blue Topaz, Iolite

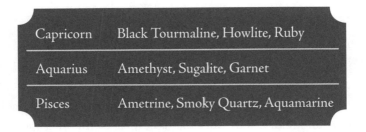

Capricorn	Black Tourmaline, Howlite, Ruby
Aquarius	Amethyst, Sugalite, Garnet
Pisces	Ametrine, Smoky Quartz, Aquamarine

There are many other possibilities that work just as well, and I suggest you find what responds best for you as an individual. I've included all twelve signs in case you'd like to use the stones for your Moon sign or rising sign. Hands-on experimentation is the best approach, so I suggest visiting crystal or metaphysical shops and rock and mineral shows when possible. Here's some information on the three I prefer for Scorpio.

Obsidian

Obsidian of any type will do, but black is best for Scorpio as it acts as a black mirror, reflecting the unvarnished truth. In addition to encouraging truthfulness, this stone helps temper intense emotions so that they can be examined with care. It also helps regulate sexual energy in the body. Obsidian increases self-control during times of great change and stress. This in turn helps you be more compassionate. It stabilizes your aura if you are under magickal or psychic attack or in an oppressive energetic atmosphere. Obsidian helps you excrete energetic or physical toxins as well.

Pale Beryl

Beryl comes in many colors, with emerald and aquamarine being the best known of this family of gems. Beryl is named after the element beryllium, which is part of the molecule that forms these crystals. Beryllium is harder than steel, lighter than aluminum, and a small amount mixed with other metals enhances their properties. Beryl that is clear or has a pale pink, purple, green, blue-green, or yellow tinting enhances the best of your Scorpio qualities. It helps you filter and sort your sensations and feelings. Pale beryl can reawaken hope and feelings of love and affection. It is soothing to the body and helps reassert the balance that is health.

Nuummite

Often called the sorcerer's stone, nuummite helps you draw in magickal power more easily and at a greater rate. It is generally black or a very dark brown with iridescent or metallic streaks and flecks. It is an ancient metamorphic stone—many of these stones are three billion years old; that calls on the hidden places deep in a Scorpio's soul. It can unlock dormant powers, memories, and recollections of past lives. Nuummite is useful as a general boost to your witchcraft, but in particular for the opening of gates, soul travel, and mediumship with some amount of protection. Nuummite helps in the removal of energies or intrusions that are not a natural part of the aura.

Intuition and spiritual guidance play a part in the making of correlations and, in the case of traditional lore, the collective experience of many generations of practitioners. There is also reasoning behind how these assignments are made, and understanding the process will help you choose well. Here are some examples of this reasoning:

🜄 Crystals assigned to Scorpio are often black, red, or deep mysterious hues to remind us of Pluto or Mars. Black tourmaline and red jasper are good examples of these.

🜄 Scorpio's metal is steel as it is an alloy that contains iron that has been transformed into something stronger. Crystals such as marcasite and chalcopyrite that contain iron, especially when mixed with other metals or carbon, are compatible with Scorpio energy.

🜄 Crystals whose lore and uses are related to Scorpio or Pluto or Mars actions or topics—such as communication with the dead, inner transformation, strong focus, and healing—are recommended for Scorpio. These include Moqui marbles or Boji stones, moldavite, and red tiger's eye.

💧 Crystals that are the opposite of the themes for Scorpio provide a counterbalance to an excessive manifestation of Scorpio traits. For example, citrine is useful for Scorpio because it is centering and brightens moods.

💧 Crystals suggested for Taurus, your opposite sign, are also useful to maintain your balance. Rose quartz is a good example of this principle.

Working with Ritual Objects

A substantial number of traditions or schools of witchcraft use magickal tools that are consecrated to represent and hold the power of the elements. Oftentimes in these systems, there is one primary tool for each of the elements and other tools that are alternatives to these or are mixtures of elements. Find and follow what works best for you. Magickal tools and ritual objects are typically cleansed, consecrated, and charged to prepare them for use. In addition to following whatever procedure you may have for preparing your tools, add in a step to incorporate your energy and identity as a Scorpio witch. This is especially productive for magickal tools and ritual objects that are connected to earth or are used to store, direct, or focus power. By adding Scorpio energy and patterning into the preparation of your tools, you will find it easier to raise, move, and shape energy with them in your workings.

There are many magickal tools and ritual objects that do not have any attachment to specific elements. The core of your life force and magickal power springs from your Scorpio Sun. So, when you consciously join your awareness of your Scorpio core with the power flowing through the tools or objects, it increases their effectiveness. Adding your watery energy does not make it a water tool, it makes it a Scorpio tool tuned to you. Develop the habit of using the name *Scorpio* as a word of power, the glyph for Scorpio for summoning power, and the greens and earthy neutral tones of Scorpio to visualize its flow. Whether it be a pendulum, a wand, a crystal, or a chalice, your Scorpio energy will be quick to rise and answer your call.

A Charging Practice

When you consciously use your Scorpio witch energy to send power into tools, it tunes them more closely to your aura. Here's a quick method for imbuing any tool with your Scorpio energy.

1. Place the tool in front of you on a table or altar.
2. Take a breath in, imagining that you are breathing in crimson or purple energy, and then say "Scorpio" as you exhale. Repeat this three times.
3. Place your hand over your sex with three fingers pointing down and spread to form an *m*. Then form a fist, put out your pinky, and swing it upward. You've just formed the glyph for Scorpio over a part of the body it rules.
4. Now using a finger, trace the glyph of Scorpio over or on the tool you are charging. Repeat this several times and imagine the glyph being absorbed by the tool.

5. Pick up the tool, take in a breath while imagining crimson or purple energy, and blow that charged breath over the tool.

6. Say "Blessed be!" and proceed with using the tool or putting it away.

Hopefully this charging practice will inspire and encourage you to experiment. Use the name *Scorpio* as a word of power, the glyph for Scorpio for summoning power, and the earthy colors of Scorpio to visualize its flow whenever you can. Feel free to use these spontaneously in all your workings. Whether it be a pendulum, a wand, a crystal, a chalice, a ritual robe, or anything else that catches your imagination, these simple methods can have a large impact. The Scorpio energy you imprint into objects will be quick to rise and answer your call.

HERBAL
CORRESPONDENCES

♏︎

These plant materials all have a special connection to your energy as a Scorpio witch. There are many more, but these are a good starting point.

Herbs	
Damiana	to stir passion and sensuality
Wormwood	for protection and uncrossing
Black Cohosh	bring courage and resolve

Flowers

Black Pansy	to quiet turbulent feelings
Asphodel	for seeing the dead and the veils
Rhododendron	strengthens openness and trust

Incense and Fragrances

Opopanax	to reveal secret knowledge
Asafetida	to repel evil and illness
Ambergris	for psychic work and dreams

CLEANSING AND SHIELDING

Zoë Howe

When meditating, practicing magic, or doing anything of that ilk, you are opening up your spiritual front door, so you want some control as to who, if anyone, comes in. At the same time, sensitive Scorps may need to armor up when we're leaving the house or scrolling through our phones. Negative influences can reach us through the content we expose ourselves to, especially if the TV is on and a newsreel kicks in. Some people can happily sit through a true crime documentary and sleep soundly directly afterward. If you're a Scorpio, this possibly does not describe you, so you need to know your limits. I'm not saying you have to limit what you watch, although some people may do well to (what goes in must come out), but we'll stand a better chance of staying stable and at peace if we at least make conscious choices.

When it comes to negative influences, we can't only consider the external, we must look within as well—usually, the main culprit when it comes to the sabotaging of our dreams is ourselves, after all. Like the image of the scorpion raising its sting and preparing to strike itself when threatened (although I have something to say about the veracity of that later), we can find ourselves hovering over the self-destruct button if we feel trapped in a negative spiral. We are all bundles of contradictions, anxieties, and shifting moods and circumstances, so bear this in mind when working to banish negativity.

Remember, if the energy that can cause chaos is within us, so is the energy that can protect us. While I always recommend connecting with protective deities and forces, protection comes from within as well as without. Draw it up within you, strengthen yourself with conviction, give yourself bones of steel. Protective warrior deities such as Astrodaddy Mars are likely to respond better to our petitions if they note that we are doing our bit, too, rather than handing over our power and looking solely outside of ourselves for help. We all contain a spark of the divine. Use this spark, develop it, and know it is linked always to the Source.

The Dark Side—and Calling In "the Team"

Let's be honest, many Scorpios are attracted to the dark side. For some of us that just means the occult. For others, it may mean something more dangerous. But it is worth remembering that there are risks on all levels of occult life, if we don't prepare ourselves properly or prioritize protection (that's a lot of p-words).

When we sit down to cast, connect, meditate, divine, or allow our unconscious thoughts—and Spirit—to come forth in our dreams, it is advisable to call in one's "team." We want our highest and best, our guardians and guides, ascended masters, soul friends, and loved ones to guide, ground, and ensure we are safe as we head into the unknown. It is my belief that our team is always there, waiting to be called on.

Building a strong and loving relationship with your team is one of the best things you can do. Not only does it remind us that we are always accompanied by those who truly love us, the more we give our team our attention, the stronger the link becomes, and the more we will receive and recognize messages through synchronicities, dreams, and all manner of other methods. Give this relationship your time, and let it be a habit to call them in and honor them. You may be blessed with the ability to hear or see them, but if you aren't, don't be disappointed—just know they are there, and they've got your back. I'll say it again: ain't no hug like a Spirit hug, and that's probably the only kind of hug *some* Scorpios would accept. (Joke. When we hug, we hug with pincers AND claws. And we might not let go.)

Our team is excellent at keeping away lower entities that might, at best, cause mischief, or mislead us during divination practices, for example. Said entities are all too ready to chime in when the Ouija board comes out. Many Scorps, especially inexperienced dabblers keen to dip a pincer into the paranormal, may be seduced by the Ouija board. This is widely regarded as a bit of a blunt instrument, usually used (unwisely) like a parlor game, or while drunk with pals in a teenage bedroom (speaking for myself, despite my mother's warnings). It's not the most respectful scenario for courting spirit communication.

The technique can be attractive because it can be apparently easy to achieve contact, but it's never guaranteed to be what you think it is or who the respondent says they are (it probably isn't Elvis or Princess Di). Another element of this kind of technique that makes it so uncertain is that what is instigating the movement of the planchette or the glass is often our own energy, or some unevolved energy close to the Earth plane that is eager to play. Allowing either of those to run rampant could also potentially block communication from higher entities whom we actually would benefit from connecting with, such as our guides.

Humans are happily fooled because we believe what we wish to be true, and we like a cheap thrill. Some people become addicted to these techniques, and I've seen strange things unfold as a result. Avoid unless you know what you're doing and are going to approach it with deep respect and proper preparation—and your team—in place. Just as you don't necessarily understand electricity but you know how to use it safely, treat communication with Spirit in the same way, and you won't risk a shock—or an all-out power cut.

Keep It Clean

I am all for putting up shields, creating circles of protection, and bringing in the light—even calling in the mighty protector Archangel Michael if I'm feeling vulnerable. (See Energy Protection and the Auric Egg on page 166 for an effective shielding technique that can be practiced daily.) However, the act of purging unwanted energy is just as important because if we don't do it, we are just enclosing unwanted energies inside our protective shell.

I'm hardline about cleansing: if I find I have retained an item or gift from an ex-lover or a false friend, I waste no time in getting rid of it. I don't want the reminder, and, more importantly, I don't want anything that links with their energy. It doesn't matter if it was an amicable breakup (yes, Scorpios are capable of those). It belongs to the past—and to a past self. Out it goes.

In terms of an energetic cleanse, I love visualization techniques and recommend using them as often as possible—it gets you into good habits of psychic hygiene and reminds you that you can call on them at any time. This can be as simple as imagining a waterfall of light pouring down on you from the heavens, and I know many people imagine the water that tumbles down upon them in the shower being white light, giving them an energetic cleanse as well as a physical one. If you have a bathtub, try the following potion bath; it will leave you feeling lighter, brighter, and clearer.

A Cleansing Potion Bath

Let's imagine you wish to have a cleansing bath that banishes unwanted energies and leaves the path clear for that which you wish to invite in. (Be intentional about all of this; ideally, write all these thoughts and intentions down.)

In terms of ingredients, I'm a big fan of using what is readily available, and you will find all sorts of things in your kitchen that will work (salt and pepper, for example). If you are fortunate enough to have a space where you can grow herbs and plants, consider what is growing naturally that is appropriate to your needs (nettle for protection, roses for love, oak leaves for strength), and harvest according to the Moon—pick plants to promote increase during the waxing or full Moon, and to support decrease and banishment during waning to dark. The new Moon is perfect for harvesting plants for initiation and new beginnings, but wait for the Witches' New Moon (when the first sliver of moonlight is visible) and definitely get an app to tell you when the Moon is void of course—you will likely struggle to get anything off the ground magically at this time. Use these periods to rest, think, and plan.

As this is a cleansing bath, we'll be working with the dark Moon. Harvest any herbs with care and a word of thanks—ask permission of the spirit of the plant and explain what you are going to do with it. Gently wash them in running water; hold and charge them with your intention.

Place them in a bowl and add any kitchen ingredients, such as cleansing vinegar, lemon juice for energy clearing, cleansing salt and protective black pepper, a pinch of cloves to nix gossip, and perhaps some flower or plant remedies, such as fringed violet (Australian Bush Flower Remedies) for psychic protection, or walnut for powerful clearing.

You could also add essential oils (perhaps rosemary for protection, lavender to heighten the frequency, or May Chang to shoo away negativity). Mix together first, or add directly to the bathwater, but make sure essential oils are diluted with a carrier oil to avoid skin sensitivities or staining. If you don't have access to any of the above, but you do have salt in the kitchen, that is more than good enough. A few cups of salt, the right words, and cast-iron belief can do much.

Be clear on your intention and speak or chant it with conviction before getting in. Submerge every part of yourself—dunk your head underneath as well. Imagine what you want to release and feel it detaching from you in the water.

Never linger in bathwater used to cleanse and banish. Get out and allow the water to drain away as you step into your new phase feeling lighter.

Other Methods of Energetic Cleansing

Smoke cleansing, by way of using incense or bundles of burning herbs, clears negativity and resets the energy of any items that come to you secondhand. We can work with the principle of cleansing with smoke and herbs by using plants that grow around us: you might have access to purifying rosemary, renewing juniper, comforting lavender, prosperity-boosting bay. If you can't access plants or trees easily, use stick or cone incense: Dragon's Blood is a favorite for banishing negativity. Take a moment to honor the spirit of the herb, make your request (purification or protection, for example) before lighting carefully and wafting the smoke wherever it is needed.

Use sound. Similar to the Chinese tradition of using firecrackers and cymbals to clear energy (and the British tradition of *wassailing*—banging pots to scare evil spirits out of the orchards), you can do anything from clapping your hands to ringing a bell to clear and reclaim your space. You can even play music. Loud. When I moved to a house with a strange past, I instinctively wanted to play exhilarating Latin music in there. I carried the stereo from room to room as I physically cleaned the place. It has felt fantastic ever since. I highly recommend cleansing via *cumbia*.

Cleansing crystals abound, some of them so high in vibration they apparently never need cleansing themselves and instantly clear the energy of anything nearby. One such stone is selenite, and I recommend placing sticks of selenite around the home. Shungite and jet are also big hitters (although jet does need cleansing); like all black stones, their clearing and protective properties are well known. The latter can be expensive, but selenite can be cheaper in its raw form and clears energy swiftly. This is also a very Scorpio way to cleanse: a silent, subtle way of perpetually protecting and cleansing, and more often than not, it hides neatly in plain sight.

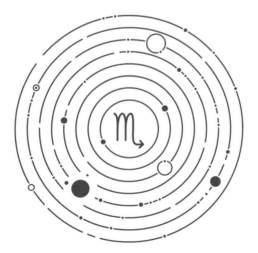

WHAT SETS A SCORPIO OFF, AND HOW TO RECOVER

Zoë Howe

Scorpio witches take everything seriously because life—and magic—is a serious business. That's not to say we don't have a sense of humor (a dark one), but our uncompromising qualities can mean that things (translation: people) often don't reach our exacting, possibly unrealistic expectations. This can be tough on us, as well as on them. Hell, we can be tough enough on ourselves in the first place, let alone anyone else. This chapter aims to pinpoint some of our flashpoints while helping us use our natural traits to turn situations around in constructive ways.

Scorpios famously never forgive or forget, which can make it challenging when working release magic—we must try to let go on every level, otherwise our brooding thoughts will undermine the magic we have worked and bring us right back to the start. Fortunately, one of the things that Scorpio is very good at is the aforementioned shadow work. We are unafraid to go to those dark, hidden places, and we are fascinated by human psychology. Admittedly, we often find ourselves turning our laser beams onto *other* people, be they irritants on social media or IRL. Before you start analyzing someone else and their behaviors, turn your focus on yourself and those inner shadow aspects that are desperate to be brought up and out into the light of conscious thought to be looked at, given your attention at last, and, yes, ultimately be either released, forgiven (we *can* do it, you know), or befriended and integrated as a hidden strength, just like our beloved stings.

Sneaks, Snakes, and Sketchy Situations

Trust is hugely important for suspicious, uncompromising Scorpio, and many of us have trust issues we find hard to heal. Part of being a human being is encountering people who range from slippery to downright sociopathic, and if our trust is betrayed, Scorpio will at best waste no more time on the perp. At worst … well, let's not go there. Call it ghosting, call it being frozen out, Scorpio knows how to bring on an Ice Age when someone tries to play us, disrespects us, or shows traits that aren't in line with our values, politics, taste in rock bands … Do we sometimes throw the baby out with the bathwater? Yes. Yes we do.

A little perspective can make all the difference. Not everything has to be wholeheartedly embraced or destroyed. We don't exactly acknowledge shades of gray, but we can save our Scorpio selves a lot of aggravation if we remember that they do exist, and also if we remember that, as I often tell myself, people are never just one thing.

What is at once a blessing and a curse is the fact that Scorpio sees beyond false charm and perceives what many others can't—and when we point it out, it can make people uncomfortable. We're like the kid in the Emperor's New Clothes—we see through people and things, and feel aghast when others can't. This kind of situation can make us second-guess ourselves, which is destabilizing and anxiety-inducing, setting us off even more. Alternatively, it can make us even more rigid in our convictions. Again, perspective is key. To quote the author Scaachi Koul, "One day we'll all be dead and none of this will matter."[1] I know people who find this phrase morbid, but I find it comforting—it helps me zoom out and away from the buttons that are getting pushed and see things for what they actually are. That said, our gift of discerning

---

1. Scaachi Koul, *One Day We'll All Be Dead and None of This Will Matter: Essays* (United Kingdom: Picador, 2017), 100.

perception must still be treasured and encouraged. These are our instincts, our Spidey senses, and like our sting, they keep us safe if we learn how to trust them.

No Justice?

Scorpio can be profoundly principled, so something else bound to get our blood boiling is the idea that so many people supposedly get away with problematic behavior, from petty slights to full-blown crime. To make matters even more infuriating, true witches and lightworkers conversely get away with very little; I believe this is because we're on an ascension path and must learn our lessons as we go. But it doesn't help when we see people merrily behaving reprehensibly without any comeback—as far as we can see. This can lead Scorpios to entertain thoughts of vengeance. Revenge is a big part of the Scorpio story, and while most witches accept that what goes around comes around, the idea that suitable justice might never be wrought is one that sets controlling Scorpio off good and proper, even prompting us to take matters into our own fiendish pincers. More often than not, this is an effective way of poisoning our own energy and wasting our own time.

As for considering vengeance for a crime committed by someone who has perhaps long since left our lives, we need to remember that, as we ourselves are evolving and developing, so may they be. We would hate it if others continued to judge us for something we did in a moment of immaturity ten years ago. We are all here to change and grow, whether consciously on a spiritual path or not. Ask yourself: Is this problem possibly out of date? Are there also things *you* did in the past that you'd never do now? Chances are those people feel similar. Chances are they've punished themselves enough. And if they haven't? Then they're not worth an atom of your energy.

Living well is the best revenge, as the saying goes. Keep that in your heart, and let it unfurl whenever you feel that instinctive pang—no matter how justified. I believe the loving, powerful forces of the divine know far better than us how situations should be dealt with, so I hand it all over and allow them to work on the bigger picture. Further entangling myself with the energy of enemies is something that I'd have to consider very carefully, and more often than not, it just isn't worth it.

There are times, however, when one might like to send someone a little message through the ether. I once did this via a piece of art, writing a letter in Morse code (again, code—*tres* Scorp) and integrating it into the artwork. This kind of energetic messaging can also be done via a technique that my fellow Scorpio witch friend Laura Keeble calls "firemail"—writing a letter, addressing it to the person, and then burning it.[2] I'd often used this method to make wishes or send messages to those in Spirit, but Laura wisely knew that the recipient didn't have to be on the other side of the veil to energetically receive a message.

Social Media Stickiness

Spirituality goes deep for serious-minded Scorpio, so it can be irritating to see someone who has never known a time other than the TikTok era of wide-open witchiness proclaiming themselves masters of the craft or putting themselves out there as authorities after having apparently discovered it ten minutes previously. Within moments they're hoovering up other people's ideas and presenting diluted versions online. Scorpio is nothing if not suspicious, but we are also protective—and possessive—of that which we value profoundly. The knowledge that someone might exploit that which we hold to be sacred is exactly the kind of thing that has us narrowing our eyes and pursing our lips in a manner that makes Professor Snape look like a Care Bear.

We can waste energy getting annoyed by things like this, but herein lies something the Scorpio witch may benefit

---

2. British artist and Scorpio witch Laura Keeble appears in my 2022 Llewellyn book *Witchful Thinking* discussing art and manifestation magic.

from working on. While you may find yourself irritated by the trivialization or posy appropriation of your way of life, check out the bigger picture, because ultimately something important is happening: the word *witch* is being presented to the mainstream world in a positive way. Its common use takes the sting out of this emotive word and makes other people want to understand it better and embrace it—or at least not fear it. Trust that this is all creating a much-needed shift in perception. The Goddess knows what she is doing, and nothing happens by accident. It also shows us that magic is everywhere, touching more people than ever in different ways, making itself known, enriching more and more lives every day. Isn't that something to celebrate?

Scorpio jealously guards that which we think is ours, so when something along the lines of WitchTok witchery gets on our wicks, watch out for when a tinge of *hey, get off my patch!* creeps in. Were you welcomed by people who had walked the path before you, people who warmly guided you when you were finding your feet? If you weren't, or if you have always been following the path privately, don't begrudge others who choose a different route—and try not to judge them if they appear to be doing it "wrong." Maybe they're just doing it differently. Are you jealous that they feel so free in sharing their practice when you felt safer keeping it under wraps? Check in with your true agenda when you feel those hackles rising. And if in doubt, get offline and mind your own business; you have your own magical practice and spiritual development to attend to, after all.

A beautiful aspect of social media is that it gives us an opportunity to connect with others like us, and share ideas in the spirit of generosity and solidarity. Witches are typically outsiders, generally misunderstood, often isolated—and totally okay with that. Swap the word *witches* with the word *Scorpios* and that sentence would work equally well. But we need to not shun community or potential kindred spirits as they come closer. Yes, there are people jumping on the bandwagon. There are also a lot of genuine people whom you may be subconsciously attracting, or whom Spirit has guided you toward, for a reason.

Attitudes of Ingratitude

Life is full of entitled takers, drains and false friends, and fragile egos. All of the above would set any sensitive person off, but for the Scorpio, even a whiff of bad manners or ego-led superiority can send us rocketing into incandescent fury. We are sensitive to others, whether we like them or not, and this means we often want to help them if we can. But, as we can't control how they respond to our efforts—if they are ungrateful, disrespectful, or otherwise don't react in the way we think they should—we easily get bogged down in righteous outrage.

When you do something for another, it's good practice not to expect credit or thanks. When we gently push our own demanding ego aside, we remember that the reward is the work and the result. Our anger may be justified but it is unlikely to change their behavior. Move on from the situation, and the person, with grace. The less we engage, the less likely the energy is to stick to us, and subsequently the less likely those characters are to appear in our lives. (Presumably to teach us how to not get bogged down with it. There are no accidents in the magical life.) Let it all fall away of its own weight. You've got Scorpio witch stuff to do.

A Scorpio's Spear-Sting

Cat Heath

As a Scorpio, it would be fair to say that I'm a little *curious* about the hidden and eldritch aspects of our deeply wondrous Middle Earth. At times, this trait can feel like dancing along the edge of a blade, a precarious balancing act between the extremes of ecstatic discovery or bloodied feet and taking a tumble. This is true Dead, Mad, or a Poet territory, and only the foolhardy go abroad without taking precautions.

In nature, scorpions have stingers to defend and turn away trouble. But as I am a pitifully stingerless human, I have to rely on tools like the spear-sting oil I give below. Anoint yourself with this to turn away trouble while you're abroad or use it on the doorposts of any building you wish to protect.

You will need:
+ Crockpot
+ 1 16-ounce bottle of olive oil
+ 3 teaspoons each of the following herbs:
    - Mugwort (against harmful spirits)
    - Vervain (known as the holiest protective herb in my birth region)
    - Nettle (a spear-carrying defender)
    - Angelica (against physical and magical attacks)
    - Hyssop (cleansing and purification)

+ Offerings for any gods/allies (if appropriate for you/your tradition)
+ A glass of water to offer to the herb-spirits
+ Tools for creating sacred space according to your tradition
+ Sieve and cheesecloth
+ Large bowl
+ Jug
+ Dark glass containers for storage (rollerball bottles are excellent when on the go)
+ Adhesive labels
+ Pen

Instructions:

Ensure your workspace and crockpot are clean and that you have everything you need. Begin by taking nine deep breaths: three to release tension, three to center yourself in the present, and three to focus on the task at hand.

Create sacred space according to your tradition and invite deities/allies if appropriate/desired. Request their help and make offerings. Call out to the herb-spirits and do the same. Set offerings aside until the oil is done, then dispose of any deity/ally offerings in your usual manner. Take the water outside and pour it onto the earth while saying prayers of gratitude to the herb-spirits.

Empty the oil into the crockpot and add each herb, chanting the charm below for each as you add it. As you chant, ensure your breath goes into the crock and visualize the oil becoming golden with its purpose and power.

Holy [herb name], aid this spell!
Be you a spear-stopper or spear-carrier,
A banisher of bane or stinging-might.
Lend your strength to this oil,
That it may turn back evil and harry harmful hands
For the good of all who use it.
So be it!

Leave the oil to infuse for nine hours on the lowest setting. Repeat the charm for each herb over the oil every three hours. Repeat a final time before turning the crockpot off. Allow to cool before handling.

Once cool, place the cheesecloth in your sieve and strain the mixture into your bowl. Use the jug and funnel to transfer into containers, then label and date your oil. Store in a cool, dark place for up to six months.

A BRIEF BIO OF BRAM STOKER

* * *

Alison Chicosky

Scorpio, ruled by both Mars and Pluto, is known for being associated with sex and death. Scorpios are often described as passionate and intense, but also resilient. Is it any surprise to learn that the author of the most influential vampire novel ever written was a Scorpio?

While Scorpio Abraham "Bram" Stoker (11/8/1847– 4/20/1912) was not, to anyone's knowledge, a witch, his name has been linked to the supernatural for over one hundred years after his death because of his famous gothic horror novel, *Dracula*. It is interesting that Vlad the Impaler was also born on November 8. While much of the world is familiar with Dracula, fewer are familiar with Bram's Stoker's life. Bram Stoker's love of stories started in his youth during which he was bedridden until the age of seven. He eventually became a theater critic and wrote several other less famous novels and short stories, as well as some nonfiction.

According to author David Skal, Stoker was queer, which was criminalized at the time. The specter of incurable syphilis also loomed over people of the Victorian era, and per Skal, was indeed responsible for Stoker's untimely death.[3] Perhaps he knew all too well the urges that compelled his character Lucy to leave her comfortable bed and seek out the dark figure whose embrace brings her closer to death.

While a Scorpio witch's affinity for occult pursuits would serve them well no matter what path they choose, inspiration can also be found in the fictional work of *Dracula* itself. Dracula not only mesmerized his fictional victims, but successfully fascinated popular culture. Though the character was fictional, some of his abilities can be cultivated by practitioners to aid in their witchcraft.

While many practitioners have heard of techniques that folks refer to as "energy vampirism" when directed at another person, drawing in vitality from an outside

3. David J. Skal, *Something in the Blood: The Untold Story of Bram Stoker, the Man Who Wrote Dracula* (United States: Liveright, 2016).

source to fuel your magic can be incredibly versatile. Two excellent sources to pull from are the Sun and the Moon.

A simple way to practice this technique involves basking in the light of one of these luminaries, drawing their power into yourself. Imagine breathing in their power as a luminous vapor filling your lungs, the light sinking into your skin, or even that your spirit is reaching out to touch the Sun or Moon. There are many possible ways to accomplish this. Focus on one that works for you, until you can feel the power filling you up.

Other techniques associated with vampires involve glamour (a type of personal illusion) and the aforementioned mesmerism. One exercise, depicted in the 1992 movie adaptation of *Dracula* involves people-watching in public places. Focus the force of your will into your gaze, and stare at a person facing away from you until they feel it and turn around. "See me ... see me now."

You can practice this by itself or combine it with the previous exercise by utilizing the solar or lunar powers you have absorbed. Focus the intensity of the Sun or pull of the Moon into your gaze, or imagine your very body shining like the Sun or Moon until you can feel it. I suspect that Bram would approve of your efforts.

A Sampling of Scorpio Occultists

NEIL GAIMAN
author of *American Gods* and *The Sandman*
(November 10, 1960)

FRANCESCA DE GRANDIS
faerie bard, witch, and author
(October 28, 1949)

FRITZ JUNG
the heart of the Witch Vox, early Pagan cyberspace
(October 31, 1952)

HILMA AF KLINT
Swedish painter and mystic
(October 26, 1862)

DAVID CHETHLLAHE PALADIN
Navajo artist, shaman, and channeler
(November 4, 1926)

ISRAEL REGARDIE
ceremonial magick adept and author
(November 17, 1907)

THE SWAY OF YOUR MOON SIGN

Ivo Dominguez, Jr.

The Moon is the reservoir of your emotions, thoughts, and all your experiences. The Moon guides your subconscious, your unconscious, and your instinctive response in the moment. The Moon serves as the author, narrator, and the musical score in the ongoing movie in your mind that summarizes and mythologizes your story. The Moon is like a scrying mirror, a sacred well, that gives answers to the question of the meaning of your life. The style and the perspective of your Moon sign shapes your story, a story that starts as a reflection of your Sun sign's impetus. The remembrance of your life events is a condensed subjective story, and it is your Moon sign that summarizes and categorizes the data stream of your life.

In witchcraft, the Moon is our connection and guide to the physical and energetic tides in nature, the astral plane, and other realities. The Moon in the heavens as it moves through signs and phases also pulls and pushes on your aura. The Moon in your birth chart reveals the intrinsic qualities and patterns in your aura, which affects the form your magick takes. Your Sun sign may be the source of your essence and power, but your Moon sign shows how you use that power in your magick. This chapter describes the twelve possible arrangements of Moon signs with a Scorpio Sun and what each combination yields.

♈

Moon in Aries

When water and fire mix under a Mars rulership, you get steam. This gives you greater drive and intensity than most Scorpios, but if the pressure gets too high, it can be dangerous. When you are at your best you are powerful, competent, and hardworking. You are resourceful and can find a way around or through any obstacle through the power of your will and self-confidence. When you are going full speed and you are not at your best, that steam may scald those near you or cause an explosion. Your next step in leveling up is about learning how to be flexible, to make compromise, and not taking offense when you are frustrated. You have the capacity for great benevolence or cruelty, and you do have a choice.

You can be warm, quirky, fun, and funny. Fairly often your life resembles a sitcom, a romcom, an epic fantasy, or some other scenario filled with dramatic possibilities. Your ethics are often situational and/or driven by your feelings for people rather than idealized rules. Your Moon and Sun are both passionate and focused on your personal goals, so what else would you expect. Try to include people more fully into your life and plans, let them in. *Lone wolf* or *brooding superhero* is a good look for you but in the long run not as satisfying. You have great sensitivity and a need for independence that can make it harder to find the right people to fill your life. They do exist, and when you make your personal life a priority, events move quickly. When in doubt, ask yourself what the kindest approach would be when dealing with those who matter to you.

An Aries Moon, like all the fire element Moons, easily stretches forth to connect with the energy of other beings. These fiery qualities help cleanse and protect your aura from picking up other people's emotional debris or being influenced by your environment. However, your Scorpio Sun loves to hang on to everything, so intentional cleansing practices are needed. When you draw in power, more will become available, and you rarely run out. You do need to be mindful of your flow and to moderate it so that you don't run too hot. The energy field and magick of an Aries Moon tend to move and change faster than any other sign, but it is harder to hold to a specific task or shape. This can be overcome with self-awareness and practice.

♉

Moon in Taurus

A Taurus Moon is opposite to a Scorpio Sun in the zodiac, and both are of the fixed modality. This can give you great perseverance but is equally likely to make you intractable because you don't want to give an inch even when it costs you more than it is worth. You have a large breadth of vision and think and plan on a grand scale. You are also a pragmatist with good common sense. Let these qualities also lead you to see the value in letting go of some details to ease restrictions in your plans. Because your Sun and Moon are opposites, it is especially important for you to find balance and the middle way between extremes. Look for omens, signs, messages, and synchronicities around you to give you guidance. The universe is always speaking to you.

This combination usually gives deep emotions, a sensual nature, a romantic heart, and a need for physical reassurance. Your energy is very attractive, so it will draw people to you whether or not you are trying. You are a charmer, and you have a compelling and persuasive effect on the people around you. When things don't go your way or your routine is disrupted, whether it is people or circumstances, you have a hard time letting go of the frustration. Seek out music, art, creative endeavors, nature, or anything else you find beautiful to get back on track.

Having dinner with friends at your home or their home is also a good idea. Trust and respect are given and earned, and you expect the same from those you let into your inner circle. When you attend to your needs and emotional well-being, you can accomplish almost anything.

A Taurus Moon generates an aura that is magnetic and pulls energy inward. This magnetic tendency is amplified by your Scorpio Sun. You are good at collecting and concentrating energy for yourself for magickal purposes. This Moon also makes it easier to create strong shields and defenses. If something does manage to breach your protection or create some other type of energetic injury, get some healing help. Generally, people with a Taurus Moon have less flexibility in their aura, but this is moderated by the water of your Sun. You can work toward improving your flexibility by leaning into the power of water. Shape-shifting and soul travel in the form of an animal may be some of your gifts.

♊

Moon in Gemini

This is a volatile and highly changeable combination with Gemini's mutability stirring up Scorpio's fixed water. You are a quick learner, which is a good thing because you want to try a bit of everything. There is always a whirlwind of activity around you as you go from interest to interest. Normally this is fine, but when you must prioritize or choose between tasks and goals, you may come to a full stop. You can see many angles and perspectives, perhaps too many, so filter your choices by what will result in something that serves you in a tangible way. You need variety in life, so your best career choices will be connected to communicating, teaching, negotiating, mental pursuits, and a fast-paced environment. Your overall perspective on life tends to be more optimistic and easier going than most Scorpios. You probably are more sociable and have a wide range of friends and associates.

Cultivating patience is essential, not just for your projects but also for how you deal with others. You are really good at rationalizing things to manage discomforts, but some type of meditation or relaxation process would be helpful. When you get too boisterous, and others say you are being too over the top, it probably means that you need a rest.

A Gemini Moon, like all the air Moons, makes it easier to engage in psychism and gives the aura greater flexibility. You have a quicksilver aura that seeks connection but not a merger with other beings and energies. When an air aura reaches out and touches something, it can quickly read and copy the patterns it finds. A Gemini Moon gives the capacity to quickly adapt and respond to changing energy conditions in working magick or using the psychic senses. However, turbulent spiritual atmospheres are felt strongly and can be uncomfortable or cause harm. A wind can pick up and carry dust and debris, and the same is true for an aura. If you need to cleanse your energy, become still and the debris will simply fall out of your aura.

♋

Moon in Cancer

With double water, your consciousness is often immersed in the flow of intuition and psychism. This gives you great insights into life and people. However, it can be stressful or disheartening, so you quickly learn to put up your shields and maintain firm boundaries. Scorpio's strong and forceful nature is redirected by this Moon into a more protective Cancerian mode of being. You will often choose to defend and nurture people close to you, causes, or institutions that you value. You may be called to become a healer and a helper in matters of physical health, mental health, or society. You aren't usually attracted to leadership positions but it is common to find yourself falling into those roles as if it were fated. You have a razor-sharp intellect and have the capacity to use logic or emotion to make your point or wriggle out of situations. As you zig and zag between reasoning and feeling, try to keep an eye on the truth and the path you wish to travel.

Intimacy, love, and a safe space to be fully yourself, especially during rough times, are essential to your long-term well-being. Yes, people will see you as ambitious and aspiring to greatness. Yes, you have the dusky, sensual energy and personal magnetism of a double water sign. However, your spirit longs for deep connection, the back-and-forth dance of romantic gestures, and falling deep into someone's soulful eyes. The two obstacles to achieving that state of union are a fear of loss masquerading as suspicion and aloof pride as a defense against revealing your shortcomings. Sharing more of yourself carries risks, but it is the surest way forward.

A Cancer Moon, like all the water Moons, gives the aura a magnetic pull that wants to merge with whatever is nearby. Imagine two drops of water growing closer until they barely touch and how they pull together to become one larger drop. The aura of a person with a Cancer Moon is more likely to retain the patterns and energies that it touches. This can be a good thing or a problem depending on what is absorbed. You must take extra care to cleanse and purify yourself before and after magickal work whenever possible. One of the gifts that comes with this Moon is a capacity for healing touch that offers comfort while filling in and healing disruptions in other people's energy. Your psychic skills are strong and would benefit from structured learning.

Moon in Leo

Both Leo and Scorpio are fixed signs, which generates a strong personality with great pride and passion. The emotional power or water and the passion and purpose of fire make you formidable and you always attract attention. Your Scorpio Sun may crave some privacy, but your Leo Moon makes that difficult. You have two default speeds, either scary fast or idling in slow circles. Pay attention when you are somewhere between those extremes so you can consciously choose those speeds. You are good at analyzing and acting in almost any arena of life. However, you have difficulty noticing when you are too forceful or brash. This may not bother you because you may think of yourself as a rugged individualist, but sometimes you unintentionally hurt people you care about. You have the capacity to lift people up or to drag them down. Make sure that the prodigious force of this combination is used in a way that matches your ideals and your goals.

You are a mixture of the brightest of lights and the deepest of shadows. This makes you especially good at uncovering secrets, finding hidden knowledge, and divining underlying causes. You are magnificent and talented in many ways, but learning to be kinder and to listen more carefully to other people is one of your life challenges. You give loyalty and expect loyalty from the people you care about. It may take some time to find the right ones. Loyalty is not enough to keep them. They need what you need, to be seen and to be appreciated. Take time to enjoy the pleasures of life but with moderation as excess is built into this combination.

A Leo Moon, like all the fire element Moons, easily stretches forth to connect with the energy of other beings. The fiery qualities act to cleanse and protect your aura from picking up other people's emotional debris or being influenced by your environment. The Leo Moon also makes it easier for you to find your center and stay centered. The fixed fire of Leo makes it easier to hold large amounts of energy that can be applied for individual and collective workings. You are particularly well suited to ritual leadership or at the role of being the primary shaper of energy in a working. Combined with your Scorpio Sun, this Moon is good for healing work, oracular work, divination, summoning spirits and powers, and past-life work.

♍

Moon in Virgo

This is one of the hardest working and deepest caring of all the Sun and Moon combinations. You love to think, study, analyze, and have clear opinions on what is right or wrong. Internally, you are reviewing and rating everything in the world around you. You tend to be a perfectionist and very focused on your work and personal projects. Though you are often good in leadership or management roles, you can find them to be tiresome and often less rewarding. Tolerance is not your strong point, but thankfully you mostly limit your comments to internal dialogue. When you do speak harshly, you can cut to the bone easily. You may be striving for perfection, but don't expect others to follow your lead on how to improve themselves. You are more modest than most Scorpios and prefer to work behind the scenes when you can. Many will think you are shy, but the truth is that you move with care, subtlety, and purpose in most settings.

You find it easier to be open with friends and partners than most Scorpios. The Virgo Moon also makes it a bit easier to maintain your emotional balance. You strive to be the stable and practical one at home and at work. You study and ponder people, feelings, nature, and society; your happiness and fulfillment depend on how you categorize and organize your findings. The story you tell yourself becomes your experience of day-to-day life. Also, the more you encourage others to think and examine their own lives, the more you will feel like you are following one of your life's purposes. It is time to take a break when you become self-indulgent or disdainful of others. These are the warning signs that you've gotten off track.

A Virgo Moon, like all the earth element Moons, generates an aura that is magnetic and pulls energy inward. This Moon also makes it easier to create strong thoughtforms and energy constructs. Virgo Moons are best at perceiving and understanding patterns and processes in auras, energy, spells, and so on. You can be quite good at spotting what is off and finding a way to remedy the situation. This gives the potential to do healing work and curse breaking among other things. The mixture of Virgo Moon with Scorpio Sun makes it easier to organize spells and rituals. You are likely to be good at creating oils, potions, and incense blends.

♎
Moon in Libra

This airy Moon with your Scorpio Sun lets you see humanity with all its flaws and still reach a positive conclusion on how you can make things better. Your intuition is strong, and you often know how to calm people, get them to open up, and listen. You are idealistic and inspirational and as the years go by you remain so, just getting a bit more pragmatic. You are not naïve; you just have confidence in your ability to make a difference. You know how to keep centered during chaos and keep both your heart and your head well balanced. You have excellent negotiating skills, though you must be mindful, or your curiosity will lead you into trouble. You do want to know everything. Your charm and winning ways will get you out of many scrapes with trouble. Libra's cardinal air pushes your Scorpio Sun to be more outgoing, fair-minded, and sensitive to the needs of others.

If you are troubled by something, it is hard for you to stop thinking about it. These thoughts can loop in your mind for days and cause additional stress without the payoff of answers or resolutions. The best way to interrupt this cycle is to do something that requires spontaneous actions. This could be playing a game, chatting with a friend, dancing, going to a social event, and so on. Shifting your focus outward will break the cycle and your subconscious can come up with useful answers. When it comes to love and friendship, you need lots of feedback to reassure you that all is well. This is not everyone's style or habit, so they may feel all is well while you are getting worried. Verbalize your needs so that they know what you need.

A Libra Moon, like all the air Moons, makes it easier to engage in soul travel and psychism and gives the aura greater flexibility. When you are working well with your Libra Moon, you can make yourself a neutral and clear channel for information from spirits and other entities. You are also able to tune in to unspoken requests when doing divinatory work. The auras of people with Libra Moon are very capable at bridging and equalizing differences between the subtle bodies of groups of people. This allows you to bring order and harmony to energies raised and shaped in a group ritual. You may have a talent for bargaining with the dead and placating or smoothing over disturbances with them or nature spirits.

♏

Moon in Scorpio

It's all or nothing with this combination because this Moon amplifies rather than moderates your Scorpio characteristics. Whether it is work, relationships, love, or hate, you will be all in and intense. You are absolutely the best in times of crisis when you become focused and cannot be swayed from accomplishing whatever needs to be done. The problem is that your "take charge" attitude that is useful in an emergency is experienced by others as unnecessary and domineering in normal times. You can be hard and proud, which can lead to combative situations. Learn to be more strategic, stand down, and save your energy for realizing your longer-term goals. Much of the work of using this combination well comes from embracing delayed gratification, not making everything personal, and spending enough time alone to reboot your emotions.

You have an astounding amount of creative energy inside you. You could be an artist, a writer, a politician, an event organizer, a religious leader, an infamous celebrity, or almost anything. It is a matter of passion, imagination, and follow-through, and you can do it. The scale of your life is also yours to decide. Some double Scorpios live lavishly in a small village their whole lives and others adventure across the world. Think well on what you truly want and move toward whatever it is. Be considerate to those who choose to be your friends or loved ones because they are choosing to cope with your stormy moods and stay. And also, be kind to the people who are not built for living in the middle of the storm and choose to leave. You crave a primal and deep closeness with a select few you let into your heart. If they don't have strong personalities with a durable sense of self-worth, they may not be a good fit for you.

A Scorpio Moon, like all the water Moons, gives the aura a magnetic pull that wants to merge with whatever is nearby. You easily absorb information about other people, spirits, places, and so on. The energy and magick of a Scorpio Moon is adept at probing and moving past barriers, shields, and wards. This also gives you the power to remove things that should not be present in healing work. This combination also makes it easier for you to imbue objects with power, spell work, or consecrations. You may have a gift for hypnosis or guiding people into trance.

♐
Moon in Sagittarius

You have an abundance of enthusiasm, optimism, and the energy to pursue your dreams and interests. You are outspoken and have a hard time bottling up your thoughts or feelings, which is unusual for a Scorpio. You are daring, curious, and love travel, and if for some reason you can't travel, you do so with your mind. This combination tends to produce a strong fascination with spirituality, religion, and the occult. You project an air of eccentricity and people feel that reality is a bit different when you are around. Remarkably, despite how good you are at understanding the world around you, you are optimistic, principled, and want to help people. You'll be more satisfied with your life if your work, paid or volunteered, is aligned with your ideals.

There are two character flaws that you must guard against. You tend to jump to conclusions before you have enough information. You also love imagining and brainstorming but creating a detailed plan and implementing it don't seem exciting to you. Work to moderate these two weaknesses and your life will improve. Sometimes your Moon gets you stuck so deep in philosophical thought that it turns into procrastination. You are healthier and happier when you are busy. You tend to be happier with friends and loved ones who give you space when needed and then love to work and/or adventure with you. You are warm and affectionate, but your habit of extreme candor can be problematic. You do have a need for freedom and a desire to explore new territories so you may settle down late in life or have many relationships. This applies to all parts of your life, inner and outer.

The auras of people with Sagittarius Moon are the most adaptable of the fire Moons. Your energy can reach far and change its shape easily. You are particularly good at affecting other people's energy or the energy of a place. Like the other fire Moons, your aura is good at cleansing itself, but it is not automatic and requires your conscious choice. The mutable fire of Sagittarius is changeable and can go from a small ember to a pillar of fire that reaches the sky. It is important that you manage your energy, so it is somewhere between the extremes of almost out and furious inferno. This aura has star power when you light it up and physical and nonphysical beings will look and listen. You can bring out the best in other beings, human or spirits.

♑
Moon in Capricorn

Capricorn Moon with Scorpio Sun generates a strong desire for power, control, and prestige. You can be warmhearted and kind, but you never lose track of whether or not you are looking after yourself. Your feelings are powerful and complicated when it comes to personal matters. You have the greatest clarity when you are thinking about your work and projects. You have great reserves of energy, intellect, and intuition. The downside to this combination is that you can be too serious and pessimistic. The longer you stay in that state of mind, the more likely you are to create trouble for yourself and others. Schedule time for recreation or it won't happen often enough. You also are prone to being too harsh a critic of your own efforts. Cut yourself some slack and you'll improve faster. You pride yourself on your poise and self-control, but if you don't relax enough, you will erupt in a memorable spiteful way.

You don't need a partner, but you generally want one. When you are in a relationship, you are passionate, protective, and attentive. The same is true with the small group of people you count as friends. You are very independent and hold to your own goals and directions, but you keep track of what is going on in the lives of the people you care about. If they need help, you will swoop in and do what you can to help. You view this assistance as a matter of honor and reciprocity. There are limits to what you can accomplish and to the regulation of your emotions. While you wish to continually improve yourself, come to terms with fact that you do have plateaus and limits. Don't forget to use your wonderfully wicked sense of humor.

A Capricorn Moon, like all the earth element Moons, generates an aura that is magnetic and pulls energy inward. What you draw to yourself tends to stick and solidify, so be wary, especially when doing healing work or cleansings. The magick of a Capricorn Moon is excellent at imposing a pattern or creating a container in a working. Your spells and workings tend to be durable. You also have a knack for building wards and doing protective magick. You have a gift for banishing negative energies and entities. With proper training, you are good at manifesting the things you need. Road opening and uncrossing work come easily to you.

Moon in Aquarius

This Moon makes you more outgoing and gregarious than most Scorpios. You have a wide range of friends and associates from many walks of life. You know what to say and when to say it to have the best impact. You can read people's reactions quickly and adjust your words and body language on the fly. This is important because in your head and heart you live several years in the future. Sometimes you don't realize that you are cutting edge, avant-garde, and that most of the people around you live in the past, not even the present. Your desire to share your views and ideas is very strong, so slow down and think before you speak, and you'll be more articulate. You can be a beacon to draw together people. You don't enjoy shallow conversations, but if you think of them as part of a process that leads to more substantial conversation, you'll tolerate the tedium better.

You prefer to be at the center of activity, so you may choose urban living. However, if you need the peace of a less congested environment, you'll need to schedule trips to cities or events to stay in touch. Another option is to up your social media and virtual game. To be more effective in winning people to your way of thinking, take more interest in their thoughts and feelings. You need to connect with both heart and mind. Your farsighted attitude makes you a bit of a rebel. Your rebellious nature also makes you sensitive, perhaps overly sensitive, to anything that feels confining or pokes at your pride. Stay flexible and wriggle out of conflicts. Wait until you can pick the time and place for difficult conversations. The persona the world sees is strong and imperturbable, but you do need support and praise. Make sure you have people who will give you a safe and caring space to be yourself.

Like all the air Moons, the Aquarius Moon encourages a highly mobile and flexible aura. This Moon works best when it is focused by the concentrated emotion of your Scorpio Sun. Grounding is important, but focusing on your core and center is more important. In this case, it is your heart center you can strengthen to stabilize your power. People with Aquarius Moon are good at shaping and holding a specific thoughtform or energy pattern and transferring it to other people or into objects. You are good at casting spells spontaneously with just a few minutes to focus.

♓

Moon in Pisces

Being a double water sign, fixed and mutable, gives psychism, emotional intelligence, and the soul of a mystic. You are imaginative, creative, a lover of beauty, and are the beating heart at the center of many clusters of friends. Although you are good at verbal communication, where you really shine is in your power to communicate with gestures, facial expressions, and the glint in your eyes. This makes you a great storyteller. Your mind and temperament make you a lifelong student of both arts and sciences. You will probably have careers in multiple fields over the course of your life. You are more prone to being giving and to self-sacrifice than most Scorpios. However, you generally don't budge an inch on your beliefs and principles at the same time you are flexible when offering assistance.

When you have not been tending to your dreams and making them a reality, you can fall into deep funks. This combo can tend toward pessimism, wallowing in emotions, and taking on the martyr role. Stop imagining all the ways things can get worse; it doesn't help. Use that profound and brilliant imagination to envision a better world—that's how it begins. Your physical health also relies on keeping yourself in equilibrium. Thankfully you have a well-developed ability to heal and regenerate, but you need real rest for this to work. In matters of the heart, you are very giving, and when you love someone, you overlook their flaws. You are a romantic; embrace it and you'll be happier. For some this will be courtship, and for others it is the romance of being alone as the witch of the woods.

With a Pisces Moon, the emphasis should be on learning to feel and control the rhythm of the energetic motion of your aura. Water Moon sign auras are flexible, cohesive, and magnetic, so they tend to ripple and rock like waves. Pisces Moon is the most likely to pick up and hang on to unwanted emotions or energies. This is made even stronger by a Scorpio Sun. Be careful, develop good shielding practices, and make cleansing yourself and your home a regular practice. Pisces Moon people are the best at energizing, comforting, and healing disruptions in other people's auras. You are also good at casting illusions, glamours, spells of stealth, and obscuration. Your Scorpio energy lets you use this Moon to find the best possible futures out of the many possibilities in divination.

TAROT
CORRESPONDENCES
Ivo Dominguez, Jr.

♏

You can use the tarot cards in your work as a Scorpio witch for more than divination. They can be used as focal points in meditations and trance to connect with the power of your sign or element or to understand them more fully. They are great on your altar as an anchor for the powers you are calling. You can use the Minor Arcana cards to tap into Mars, Sun, or Venus in Scorpio energy even when they are in other signs in the heavens. If you take a picture of a card, shrink the image and print it out; you can fold it up and place it in spell bags or jars as an ingredient.

Scorpio Major Arcana
Death

All the Water Signs
The Ace of Cups

Scorpio Minor Arcana

5 of Cups	Mars in Scorpio
6 of Cups	Sun in Scorpio
7 of Cups	Venus in Scorpio

• MY MOST SCORPIO WITCH MOMENT •

Zoë Howe

I t's not for nothing that we are known as the quiet ones, the mysterious ones, the mean and moody rock stars of the zodiac. Dark glasses on (to shield that powerful gaze), we are the cool, inscrutable bass player, sexily silhouetted at the back of the stage rather than the showy lead singer posturing at the front. We are the murder-mystery writer, rather than the TV showbiz journalist. We like to let people work things out for themselves rather than hand everything over on a plate.

That, however, doesn't mean we don't notice when other people could do with a little Scorpio magic (best to do so with their consent, natch). The following examples relate directly to menstruation, and while I am well aware that not everyone menstruates, the principle behind the witchery inherent in these stories can relate to any area of our personal lives. It's ultimately all about will and control. We can't control everything (no, Scorpio, not even you can do that).

But we can certainly control more than we have been led to believe, if we try.

Moontime Maneuvers and the Power of Deciding

Like many children, I had an easy relationship with "magic," although I wouldn't have called it that at the time. I didn't question that I could work with energy with my mind and will, bending and stretching situations to suit certain needs. It's usually when we get older that we need to be reminded of what our minds are capable of, but back then, and certainly around my tweenage years—classically a period (no pun intended) charged with psychic energy, I found that the power of decisive thought could be sufficient to bring about favorable effects.

Now, being a child, sometimes what I thought would be a favorable effect at that time would be something I'd regret in the future, such as deciding that I no longer wanted to grow in height. Aged ten, I was the tallest kid in class and was feeling increasingly self-conscious. My wish was granted, even though I have a tall father, an average-height mother, and a sister who is a good head and shoulders taller than me. No doubt anxiety played a part in charging my intention— emotion is key in getting things done magically.

Full disclosure: I do *occasionally* wish, as an officially short adult, that I hadn't done that now. Still, my petite stature is part of my identity; I mostly love it and the main thing is that this story reminds me what a determined Scorpio witch can do when we put our minds to something. If I could talk to that girl now, I'd gently suggest not standing in the way of nature in this case, and encourage her to embrace what might have been an elegant, willowy physique, but either way, I have to take my hat off to her. That kid knew how to get results.

Here's another example of this approach, but one that has served me consistently rather better in my adult life, and one that is very Scorpio in its association with sexual regions and dark, hidden places, not to mention the themes of death and rebirth, which pertain to the menstrual cycle—not that I would have been aware of that at this point in my life. Aged eleven, I made the decision to have good periods. I realize this may seem ridiculously simplistic and probably irritating to people who experience debilitating periods; all I can say is this is what happened, and I am sharing it with you to, again, prove a point, because this happy result was not necessarily my destiny—it was definitely not in my genes. That's one childhood decision I definitely don't regret, and I always feel grateful for the relatively easy time I have each month. This doesn't mean I make a point of going disco-dancing in hot pants or cycling around in white jeans like someone in a tampon advert every month—I respect the flow and rest and retreat, reflecting nature and what this process symbolizes— but it does mean that I am able to feel happily in tune with the shifts of my body without feeling angry or distracted by excruciating pain. Even as a child, I do remember also feeling privately quite enchanted by menstruation; I felt it was magical somehow, and I felt inspired to write some really bad poems about it—entirely in code so no one else could read them. Yep, I know. Blood, sexuality, and secret codes. We're talking *peak* Scorpio.

We may be less in tune with the Source as adults, but that doesn't mean we can't still make these decisions for ourselves with consistent effort and see what happens. The main thing is, as ever, to try. If we find there is resistance to our magical decision-making, there may be shadow aspects that need some gently determined and compassionate work, so go within, face them, journal about them, and see what comes up. Request guidance in your dreams if you are unclear on where to start. If you're anything like me, all sorts of interesting things will start emerging from your unconscious and queuing up for your attention! This may feel like a lot, but it's important, it's an act of self-love, and it's liberating. It's also never-ending, so you may as well find a way to enjoy it.

(Scorpio, knowing you like I do, I know you'll enjoy it more than most.)

In later years there would be another occasion of a moontime maneuver, this time on behalf of two friends of mine. At this time, I was part of a theater company as an actor, and the company was on tour in Ireland, a place full of ancient magic and one that has strong family resonance for me. Whether this connection helped charge what I was about to do with extra efficacy, I don't know. Again, full disclosure, I was young, not terribly focused, inexperienced, and not in full control of my magic. I just did what I did, and I probably wouldn't do it again in such an offhand way, because one never knows what the results will be down the line. That said, I had been reading the works of ethics witch Marion Weinstein, which had armed me with more caution and caveats than I had previously been aware of. I can also say that I am not aware of either of the individuals involved having had any problems since. Still, I include this as a Scorpio witch moment because it involves blood, it involves sex, and it involves diamond-strong determination. I hope that some of the Irish wise women of yore, well-versed in women's issues, stepped in to ensure the safety of this impromptu working; we can and should request and honor the assistance of those who walked the paths before us wherever appropriate. Never forget that they are there, and they may well connect when your working chimes with the magic they themselves worked in life. Sometimes I am reminded of this beautiful and powerful continuum in very moving and exciting ways: the feeling of a hand holding mine in circle, for example, or the perception of spirit lights at pertinent moments—little flickers or dots of white or colored light flashing around me, or another person (and yes, I've had my eyes tested). Back to the story.

While on tour, I remember getting ready for a show in the dressing room with two of the other female actors, whom I'll call Clodagh and Amber. I can see them now, sitting in front of the mirrors, talking about their boyfriends who were due to come out to Ireland and visit them. They were complaining because Amber's boyfriend was coming next week, when her period was due. Clodagh's boyfriend was due the next day, when *her* period was due. "Oh, I'll just swap them round for you," I said, jokingly (sort of). We all laughed. But then I did it.

Whether or not I really believed this would be successful, I can't remember, but I did still have a natural trust in what was possible. I silently and sincerely requested for this swap to happen, *if it was for their highest good*, and that the timing of their flow would be perfect, ensuring that they could enjoy their time with their respective beaus to the fullest. I then positioned my index fingers parallel to each other, pointing at each of the women, and then once I had sent off my thought, I swiftly moved the fingers in their opposite directions, to indicate a swapping. This felt like the right thing to do, and also was a bit of symbolic theater, although by this time I'm not sure anyone was still paying any attention; the women were back to concentrating on applying their makeup (we had a show to do, after all). But lo and behold, it would transpire that the timings of their periods did indeed swap, leaving them free to have fun with their beloveds unimpeded by sanitary towels, pain, and, well, flow. They were amazed—I think I was too—but it was also another reminder to me that we have rather more power over how things go for us than we have often been conditioned to believe, whether by mundane life, by limiting beliefs passed on by others, or by the patriarchal society in which we live. We can live in the world but still opt out of limited ways of thinking and blend our creativity, ever-growing knowledge, and intuition to find solutions. When we do this, incredible possibilities can open up to us.

YOUR RISING SIGN'S INFLUENCE

Ivo Dominguez, Jr.

The rising sign, also known as the ascendant, is the sign that was rising on the eastern horizon at the time and place of your birth. In the birth chart, it is on the left side of the chart on the horizontal line that divides the upper and lower halves of the chart. Your rising sign is also the cusp of your first house. It is often said that the rising sign is the mask you wear to the world, but it is much more than that. It is also the portal through which you experience the world. The sign of your ascendant colors and filters those experiences. Additionally, when people first meet you, they meet your rising sign. This means that they interact with you based on their perception of that sign rather than your Sun sign. This in turn has an impact on you and how you view yourself. As they get to know you over time, they'll meet you as your Sun sign. Your ascendant is like the colorful clouds that hide the Sun at dawn, and as the Sun continues to rise, it is revealed.

The rising sign will also have an influence on your physical appearance as well as on your style of dress. To some degree, your voice, mannerisms, facial expressions, stance, and gait are also swayed by the sign of your ascendant. The building blocks of your public persona come from your rising sign. How you arrange those building blocks is guided by your Sun sign, but your Sun sign must work with what it has been given. For witches, the rising sign shows some of the qualities and foundations for the magickal personality you can construct. The magickal personality is much more than simply shifting into the right headspace, collecting ritual gear, lighting candles, and so on. The magickal persona is a construct that is developed through your magickal and spiritual practices to serve as an interface between different parts of the self. The magickal persona, also known as the magickal personality, can also act as a container or boundary so that the mundane and the magickal parts of a person's life can each have its own space. Your rising also gives clues about which magickal techniques will come naturally to you.

This chapter describes the twelve possible arrangements of rising signs with a Scorpio Sun and what each combination produces. There are 144 possible kinds of Scorpio when you take into consideration the Moon signs and rising signs. You may wish to reread the chapter on your Moon sign after reading about your rising sign so you can better understand these influences when they are merged.

♈

Aries Rising

This is a forceful combo with high aspirations and tons of energy, but you need to be careful not to burn out. You may not run out of energy, but you will get too crispy around the edges from this fire if you don't learn to rein yourself in. You are more fitness focused and physically active than most Scorpios. Be cautious that you don't overindulge in life's physical pleasures because you are drawn to excess. You can also come across as too forceful and impetuous, so take care that you don't create pointless drama. Take it down a notch or you'll be frustrated by the outcomes.

You secretly enjoy conflict, but be aware that other approaches may serve you better.

Mars is Aries' ruling planet and is Scorpio's second ruler after Pluto. This combination makes you quick, decisive, incisive, and you radiate a vitality that attracts others. Your friends and partners need to be resilient and energetic to keep up with you. Take some time to think before jumping into new friendships or relationships. Your appearance and how you carry yourself do not reveal all your internal state, so you often say things that surprise people. Physical activity is important to maintain your physical health and to blow off steam.

An Aries rising means that when you reach out to draw in power, fire will answer faster and more intensely. Use your Scorpio fixed water with fire to create a great deal of magickal power. This combination makes it easier for you to summon and call forth spirits and powers and create bindings. The creation of servitors, amulets, and charms is favored as well. This rising amplifies protective magick for yourself and others. You are able to sense trouble long before it is evident to others and come up with countermeasures quickly.

♉

Taurus Rising

A Taurus rising can bring serenity and steadfastness that complements Scorpio's passionate nature. You have a greater need for quiet times and a cozy home than most Scorpios. You seem easygoing and placid on the outside, but your internal world is stormy and filled with plans for your actions. You are practical and very resolute in working toward your goals. Sometimes you maneuver people so well they hardly complain when you get what you want. However, if your anger comes out, the power of two fixed signs comes out in full force. Taurus loves safety and Scorpio revels in taking risks, and you swing back and forth between these two modes of being.

You are a thorough and conscientious worker and especially good at organizing tasks and managing people. You don't really care about money so much as what it can do for the quality of your life. It is easier for you to talk about other people's emotions, but you are shy when it comes to expressing yours. You are extremely loyal and loving, but don't expect your friends or partners to match you in this regard. People show love, affection, and loyalty in different ways. As you get older, try to maintain or increase your level of physical activity to lift up your vitality and to keep your body comfortable.

Taurus rising strengthens your aura and the capacity to maintain a more solid shape to your energy. This gives you stronger shields and allows you to create thoughtforms and spells that are longer lasting. This combination makes it a bit harder to call energy, but once it is started, the flow is strong. You have a powerful gift for invocations, trance work, and hypnosis. This combo also makes it easier to work with nature spirits and plant spirits in particular. Spells to reveal the truth or what is hidden work well for you.

♊

Gemini Rising

This rising sharpens your communication skills and makes you a compelling writer or speaker. You are more inquisitive about everything and everyone than most Scorpios. This combination makes you a bit of a loner who also wants to be involved in society. The internal struggle and contradictions are the root of much of your motivation. You move from interest to interest with great energy and must strive to finish one thing before beginning the next. If something is a mystery, you're even more intrigued. Eventually you'll narrow your list of activities and accomplish more. Your sense of humor and love of the absurd will help smooth the way.

You come across as bright, sometimes edgy, and genuinely interested in the people around you. You tend to treat your friends as if they were family and your family as if they were friends. Usually this works, but when it doesn't, quickly adjust how you see and treat the person who doesn't like this arrangement. You love to tease and be playful one minute and then dead serious the next. You love frequent change in your home, social life, and work and you'll need friends and partners who are comfortable with this. Recognize that you can be a bit overwhelming, and you'll be more understanding.

Gemini rising combines your Scorpio mind to make you adept at writing spells and rituals that make good use of invocations and symbols. This rising helps your energy and aura stretch farther and adapt to whatever it touches. You would do well to develop your receptive psychic skills as well as practices such as mediumship and channeling. You may have a gift for interpreting dreams and the words that come from oracles and seers. This combination often has a knack for knowing how best to use music, incense, crystals, and props in magick.

Cancer Rising

The cardinal water and fixed water of your rising and Sun cause you to experience the world primarily through your emotions. You have a hard outer shell to defend, which is good because you tend to seek out tests and challenges. You are more easily hurt than most Scorpios, though you still manage to shine and seem untroubled. You are so good at masking what you feel and think that most think you are an open book. You also keep secrets well and are good as a confidante. You want to go with your gut most of the time, but that is not a good idea. Choose to use your intellect so you are not ruled by your emotions. An even mix of head and heart will steer you right.

You have an aptitude for making money, managing other people's money or resources, and business in general. If that does interest you, then you may be called to one of the sciences or a career that uses your innovations in the reuse or upscaling of resources. As the years go by, your life gets better and your status rises. Your success in relationships is directly correlated to developing skill at regulating your emotions. Your gut and digestive health is strongly affected by your emotional state; use it as an indicator to attend to your distress.

Cancer grants the power to use your emotions, or the emotional energy of others, to power your witchcraft. Though you can draw on a wide range of energies to fuel your magick, raising power through emotion is the simplest. You have a gift for clairvoyance, scrying, and animal communication. Moon magick for practical workings for abundance or healing of the heart comes easily for you. Color magick, such as the choice of colors for candles, altar cloths, robes, banners, and color visualization, can also serve you well.

♌

Leo Rising

The fixed strength of your Sun and rising makes you a formidable and flamboyant individual. You have a deep confidence in your ability to do what would be impossible for many others. You constantly strive to manifest success in all its forms. You do best when you are in charge or working solo. You are your own worst judge at times and need to have people who will help you enjoy what you achieve. One of your challenges is that you have many talents and are torn about which ones should be your focus. Light and dark are equally present within you and you must find the middle between the two. *Love* and *dignity* should serve as the keywords to guiding your choices.

You are a loyal friend and tend to forgive offenses swiftly, though you never forget them. Be as kind to yourself as you are to others. In matters of love and friendship, you have power, appetites, and passions that must be fulfilled. In personal matters, your hardest lesson is to learn that being at peace is more important than being right. Outwardly you look confident, but internally you have many worries and doubts. Be patient as those close to you get to see and understand your inner self. You prefer quality over quantity in most things in life.

Leo rising means that when you reach out to draw in power, fire will answer as easily as water. Focus on the flexibility in your energy and imagination to access the other elements. Your aura and energy are brighter and sturdier than most people's, so you attract the attention of spirits, deities, and so on. Whether or not showing up so clearly in the other worlds is a gift or a challenge is up to you. Your Sun and rising give you a knack for healing and transformative work.

♍

Virgo Rising

Virgo's mutability and earthiness add some flexibility and practicality to your Scorpio ardor and fervor. Your powers of observation and reasoning are very keen and your desire to learn and investigate is almost boundless. You aspire to perfection, and you work so hard that that goal to be the best seems almost possible. In your personal life and your work life, be watchful against focusing on the flaws and errors. You can get caught up in some nonproductive cycles of thoughts and feelings. It is extremely hard for you to ask for favors or accept help that is freely given. This is one of your most serious weaknesses.

You love your interests and projects as much as, maybe more, than you do people. So, to have successful close relationships, you need people who are comfortable with the amount of space you need. Ideally, they also have many projects of their own to keep them occupied when you are focused elsewhere. It is also important to know that sometimes you do have to bend or break the rules for better outcomes. Don't turn small glitches into major problems; try to maintain a sense of proportion in your relationships. When you are stressed out, you can convince yourself that you are sick and eventually manifest illness.

Virgo rising with a Scorpio Sun makes it easier to work with goddesses and gods who are connected to the element of earth, plant life, animal spirits, or death work. You have a knack for creating connections between different kinds of magick and making them combine. Magickal research, divination, oracular work, and healing work are favored by this combination. Be careful when you entwine your energy with someone else's because you can pick up and retain their patterns and issues. Always cleanse your energy after doing solo or collective work. Adapting old rituals or magickal methods to modern times is one of your talents.

♎

Libra Rising

Your Libra rising is outgoing and extroverted, and your Scorpio Sun is more introverted and wants privacy. It is best if you can find the midpoint between these extremes because if you don't, your behavior will pendulum back and forth. You are more focused on relationships than most Scorpios and will develop excellent people skills. You feel that part of your work is building lasting harmony and understanding. This is how you want to make your mark in the world. You do this by teasing deep issues to the surface with seemingly casual conversation. You know how to bide your time and act at the right moment.

A messy or unlovely room can dampen your mood as fast as an impolite person. The reverse is also true in that beauty feeds you. Make sure the spaces you occupy are as harmonious and lovely as you can manage. Friendships and romantic relationships are sacred to you, and you expect much from those you hold dear. Despite that, you can be aloof and cold when you are offering advice that seems reasonable and sound to loved ones. Unfortunately, it may be experienced as being harsh because it lacks your standard ease, warm emotions, and grace. Show your heart when you need to point out problems.

Libra rising with a Scorpio Sun wants to express its magick through carving and dressing candles, creating sumptuous altars, writing beautiful invocations, or creating amazing ritual wear. You also know how to bring together people who use different types of magick and arrange smooth collaborations. You are good at spell work for making peace, laying spirits to rest, attracting familiars, and fostering self-love. Working with sound in magick and healing—whether it be voice, singing bowls, percussion, or an instrument—is also one of your gifts. You are especially good at performing rites of passage.

♏

Scorpio Rising

Being a double Scorpio puts your charisma, air of mystery, and personal power off the charts. You live in the moment, but you want to know all the details and backstory that lead to each moment. When you are at your best, you are the brightest light or the darkest shadow in the room. If you feel blocked from reaching your goals, this combination can lead you to be seen as domineering or insensitive. Compromise does not come easily to you, but sarcasm does. You are an expert at asking questions and listening deeply but can't stand superficial matters. When you give your heart to love, friendship, or a purpose, you do it fully and with great vigor. You can be a stalwart ally and defender, especially when the odds are not in your favor.

You have impressive self-control until you don't. It would be wise to cultivate ways to notice when you are about to blow up and find some solitude to cool off. Success in your work life depends on having backup plans for when you hit the wall. This much Scorpio and water creates an internal tension between being cruel or kind, open or secretive, affectionate or aloof, and so on. Turn these tensions into shades of gray or, better yet, a full rainbow to access your power.

Scorpio rising makes your energy capable of cutting through most energetic barriers. You can dissolve illusion or bring down wards or shields and see through to the truth. You may have an aptitude for breaking curses and lifting oppressive spiritual atmospheres. You could be a seer but only if you learn emotional detachment. You have a knack for spells related to transformation, finding hidden or lost things, and revealing past lives. It is important that you do regular cleansing work for yourself. You are likely to end up doing messy work and you do not have a nonstick aura. You would do well as a death midwife or a psychopomp.

↗

Sagittarius Rising

This rising's enthusiasm and vision combined with your Sun's need for depth can make you great at whatever you choose to do. You also don't rest on your laurels for long before you get back to work. The relentless Sagittarius energy makes you more outgoing and playful than most Scorpios. You love to travel and are equally interested in cultures, landscapes, and meeting new people. You have an unquenchable energy that is powered by optimism and vision. You love work almost as much as play so keep an eye on the balance between your personal life and work. When you need to recharge fast, go outdoors; being outside lets you feel the interconnectedness of all living things.

Sagittarius wants freedom and adventure in relationships and Scorpio is often possessive and wants stability. Whether it is friends or lovers, find the right proportion of these two ways of being. It is likely that you can turn off your emotions for the sake of clarity and efficiency. This is useful, but it may cause you to worry that you are coldhearted.

This is not true unless you choose to always throttle back your feelings. Let the people you care about know what is going on when you pull back.

Your magick is stronger when you are near fire or water. This could be a candle or a bowl of water, but a bonfire or a body of water is even better. Your rising sign's fire can become any shape or size you need. Skill in the use and creation of ritual tools is favored by this combination because you can push your energy and intentions into objects with ease. You have a talent for rituals and spells that call forth creativity, wisdom, and freedom. If you do astral travel or soul journeying, be sure all of you is back and in its proper place within you. You also are good at seeing through deceptive or stealth magick.

♑

Capricorn Rising

Serious, obsessive, and goal oriented is just a normal day for you. You embrace struggles and challenges and laugh at obstacles because you get a great amount of satisfaction in proving your strength and merit. If you are not active and striding toward your goals, you begin to doubt yourself. Capricorn's earth keeps your watery emotions underground, but that water is highly pressurized. Learning to compromise is doubly a challenge because neither Capricorn nor Scorpio is fond of doing so. Also, please restrain your urge to smite your enemies. Your carefully crafted network of connections and favors can be undone by rash outbursts.

When you take a positive interest in specific people, it can be mutually beneficial. You tend to be a stabilizing influence in the lives of those you interact with. You are a good role model for perseverance and outcome setting. In matters of love or close friendship, do not let worry over loss prevent you from sharing yourself with others. The majority of the time, you are an excellent judge of character and intentions. Also, those close to you do not judge you as severely as you do yourself; in that, you are often pessimistic. Remind yourself of the manners and the rules of society to keep you in check when you are running too hot or feel out of control.

Capricorn rising creates an aura and energy field that is slow to come up to speed but has amazing momentum once fully activated. Try working with crystals, stones, even geographic features like mountains as your magick blends well with them. Your rituals and spells benefit from having a structure and a plan of action. Multipart spells done over time are often your best work. You are especially good at warding and spells to make long-term changes. You may have a commanding voice that the spirits hear.

Aquarius Rising

You are definitely quirkier and more eccentric than other Scorpios; you'll always be memorable. You see the world very differently, and this gives you an off-beat sense of humor. You also get joy from finding ways to circumvent the rules in the game of life. You have lots of areas of special interest, so the terms *geek* or *nerd* are probably appropriate and proudly claimed. You may appear to be a bit cold, but you do care deeply about the state of the world. Although you are forward-thinking, your desire for certainty and purity in your beliefs and ideologies can get in the way of progress. Although you dislike being restricted, you often have the urge to restrict others.

This combination makes for original thinking and moments of genius in the arts or sciences. You may have a gift for technology or information management. Your expressive and creative speech makes it easy to connect with people. It is harder for you to go from casual friendship to something deeper because you need to drop your act. This is hard because you are always on the alert, a bit hypervigilant, looking to avert trouble. You enjoy traveling as much as you do kicking back at home. Friends and partners you can do both with are keepers.

Aquarius rising helps you consciously change the shape and density of your aura. This makes you a generalist who can adapt to many styles and forms of magick. Witchcraft focused on increasing intuition, analysis of problems, and release from emotional restrictions is supported by this combination. Visualization can play an important role in your magick and meditations. If you aren't particularly good at visualization, then focus the spoken word to tune in to your power. Aquarius rising is gifted at turning ideas into reality. You have a gift for spells that have tangible real-world results quickly.

♓

Pisces Rising

Your Pisces-inspired psychic perceptions connect you with other people's feelings and thoughts. You are guided and often protected, but don't make your spirit helpers work too hard. You are doubly mysterious and enigmatic with fixed and mutable water. People are never quite sure what to expect as there is an almost mystical haze around you. Those you count as family, you will defend until your last breath. Your changing moods can be a challenge to your loved ones; recognize that and be kind. Those you disapprove of will discover your gentle exterior is camouflage for your wicked sting. When you've judged someone, your opinion rarely changes.

You can excel in a wide range of fields, but the ones that make you feel alive involve providing people with an experience that opens their hearts, minds, or spirits. You feel like your talents are wasted when your creativity is not recognized. Spirituality, magick, and religion have a profound impact on you and are involved in many of the turning points in your life. Faith in yourself or something greater is the source of your capacity to endure and persevere. Music, and the arts in general, is the best medicine for your body, mind, and spirit.

Pisces rising connects your Scorpio Sun with the other planes of reality. Your power, as a witch, flows when you do magick to open the gates to the other worlds. You have a special gift for creating sacred space and blessing places. You can do astral travel, hedge riding, and soul travel in all its forms with some training and practice. You can help others find their psychic gifts. Mental training to sharpen your powers of concentration is essential for you to reach your potential. Meditation, memory exercises, and visualization practices serve you well.

A DISH FIT FOR A SCORPIO: SENSATIONAL BLACKBERRY AND BRIE SANDWICH

Dawn Aurora Hunt

* * *

This sandwich contains surprising flavor combinations that will seduce the tastebuds with hints of thyme, tart blackberries, and the undeniable allure of melted cheese.

Scorpio, you are no stranger to deep emotional and spiritual sensations. What's more is that sharing these intimate moments with others helps you feel closer to them. As you are no ordinary Sun sign, this sandwich is no ordinary dish. Luxurious and seductive flavors like blackberries and creamy Brie cheese are melted and married in this completely sharable dish, bringing energies of lustful wanting and joyful nurturing for deep connectivity on the emotional and metaphysical plane. Make this dish to share with a partner, lover, or close friend to deepen your bonds and draw them into your desires, whether they are romantic or otherwise.

Note: If your diet precludes you from eating meat, simply omit the prosciutto from this recipe. If you are unable to tolerate gluten or wheat, you can easily substitute this bread for a gluten-free alternative.

Ingredients:

+ 4 tablespoons butter, softened
+ 1 teaspoon fresh thyme, chopped
+ 1 teaspoon fresh parsley, chopped
+ 1 large loaf of sourdough bread sliced into large, long slices
+ 4 ounces blackberry preserves
+ 4 ounces fresh blackberries
+ 8 ounces creamy Brie cheese, chilled and sliced as evenly as possible
+ 4–6 thin slices of prosciutto (optional)
+ 4 ounces baby arugula

Directions:

In a small bowl, mix butter, thyme, and parsley. Spread the butter mixture on one side of four slices of bread. Heat a large skillet to medium heat. Place two slices of bread, butter side down, on the warm skillet. Layer the bread with two to three slices of Brie cheese then small dollops of blackberry preserves. Add the blackberries, about four to six berries per sandwich. After about two minutes the Brie will start to soften and melt. Layer on a small handful of arugula leaves and a slice of prosciutto if using and an additional two pieces of cheese. Top with another slice of bread, butter side out. Flip the whole sandwich over in the pan using a large spatula and heat until all cheese has melted and the bread has turned golden brown. Remove from heat and enjoy warm.

RECHARGING AND SELF-CARE

Zoë Howe

Scorpio has such indomitable energy that, unless we are careful, we risk burning out. We get addicted to challenges and are obsessive in our approach to pretty much everything we take on. With this in mind, here's a motto I like to keep up my sleeve: just because you can, doesn't mean you should. We know Scorpio can have extraordinary energy levels and formidable staying power. We dare ourselves to surmount ever greater heights, competing with that last version of ourselves, powering ahead ... and sometimes we're not even sure exactly why other than to prove to ourselves, and maybe others, that we can. Remind yourself before you say yes yet again: *just because I can, doesn't mean I should.*

The *sleep when I'm dead* vibe rarely makes sense for the magical practitioner. We are usually sensitives by nature, empaths who need to periodically restore and reflect. Be in nature, look at the sky, get some perspective. If an opportunity presents itself for you to just be, take that opportunity.

Embracing the Sting

Scorpios are healers, and we are willing to go through the darkness to do the work, but we must ensure that we use that healing for our own purposes as well as those of others. All too frequently we do the opposite: self-critical to a fault, our unforgiving sting is too often turned inward onto the self when we don't meet our own exacting standards. We must work on being our own best friends—and that means befriending *all* our aspects. That means including the sting. No matter what you've been told, how you've been encouraged to hide it, or whether you feel it represents a toxic trait that you'd rather wasn't there, when we work to embrace, respect, and appreciate that lethal stinger, we give it the role it really wants: to protect us.

Meditate upon that idea. Invite yourself to allow the ultimate Scorpio symbol—the one that strikes fear and aversion into the hearts of apparently everyone—to bless, empower, and guard you. See it like a backbone, a core of inner strength, a shield as well as a weapon. Reassure your sting, integrate it. Be proud of it! Never mind what other people say. "Uh-oh, Scorpio! Sting in the tail!" Just say, "That's right, honey. And I know how to use it." They'll think you're joking. But you *should* know how to use it—and that doesn't mean forgetting it's there until a situation arises, only to lash out in a destructive way. It means honoring it, trusting it to have your back—literally—and deploying it with precision, wisdom, and finality when required.

I can think of many occasions when being in touch with my sting would have given me the protection I sorely needed. Thanks to societal conditioning (*Be nice and sweet! Be more friendly! Give your uncle a hug! Smile!* etc.), I felt uncomfortable as a youngster about this sting aspect that no one wanted to be near. I felt as if I had to compensate for it with extra niceness because surely I must be some kind of monster underneath it all. Inevitably this temporarily damaged my natural-born Scorpio witch instincts, which were actually very sharp, and very strong. Muffling these gifts was confusing—and unwise. I have always loved being a Scorpio but, like so many women from my generation and before, from girlhood I took on messaging that I translated thus: bury that sting—remove it if possible. I was missing the point, no pun intended. What I was also doing was something far bigger and more damaging than simply trying to damp down an astrological trait. I was actively denying my power, throwing it away in case it frightened other people, and putting myself at risk as a result. The irony is that when you see someone with a strong, healthy, fierce sense of self-empowerment, it's not frightening at all. It's inspiring. There'll be those who are threatened by it (hi patriarchy!), but those people don't matter at all, even though they've been generally the ones in charge for hundreds of years. They've had it their way for long enough, and yes, people like us are going to make them feel uncomfortable. This is a good thing.

When I suppressed the sting, I went against my nature and ended up being more open than I should have been because I had been led to believe I'd be rejected otherwise. Not only did this mean I ignored those instincts, my Scorpio sensitivity meant I was more hurt than some other signs might have been by what inevitably ensued. So, to paraphrase the *Dr. Strangelove* subtitle, learn to stop worrying and love your sting, if you haven't already. You will feel more complete, stronger, safer, more in control, and deeply respectful of yourself. Let them fear your sting if they're silly enough not to understand its true integrity. Don't go to the other extreme and start lashing it about, but do understand how it can help you, and—this goes out to the female/working-class/non-white/ LGBTQIA+/nonbinary Scorpio witches in particular—*learn how to use it.*

Scorpio Solitude

Scorpio needs alone time, and the use of social media is largely at odds with this aspect of our true nature. While we understandably can feel we need to be connected rather than not—especially in this, the age of connectivity—it inevitably makes us a little uncomfortable. Scorpio witch is unlikely to be too at home spending all their time showing off online, although the seductive nature of the digital world can hook us in. But while we might struggle with our own, often addictive, personalities when it comes to the internet, we know that the (magical) work is the thing. To conduct that work secretly, and then to see it manifesting—and being the only one who knows its origins—is deeply satisfying to a Scorpio. The purity of working this way—i.e., without having exposed our workings or intentions to others—is a potent part of the practice.

Solitude is essential to achieve the above, not just when it comes to magical work, but in order to feel in balance at all. We suffer if we don't insist upon privacy as often as we need it. Naturally depending on our circumstances, privacy isn't always possible, but we are at our best when we have carved out at least a few moments for ourselves. I keep returning to the theme of death and rebirth, but it is so key for Scorpios: we need to retreat into the comforting darkness of our symbolic caves—our own personal Hades—before being born anew when we are ready.

Scorpio naturally likes to do everything without asking for outside help, but we can't always do it all alone. Remember, you can call upon your higher Self, your soul, and your spirit team when you need strength and solace. And, hey, you can even call on other people too. In fact, I recommend it—no witch is an island (even a Scorpio witch), so allow others in sometimes, and don't be too judgmental if they aren't basically *you* in another human form. It is good to feel supported by community, and working magic with others for a shared intention is naturally powerful. Admit you don't know everything and that you can learn from others, whether you work solitaire or as part of a coven.

Taking Care of You

Scorpio is excellent at setting boundaries and conjuring up protection, whether via our own sheer will or by working with the warrior energy of our corresponding deities (which can include Hecate, Kali, Durga, the Morrigan, Lilith, Set, and, of course, Mars and Pluto). But, when it comes to taking care of ourselves, are we always as stringent as we could be?

Despite the not exactly cuddly image, Scorpios love deeply, are loyal to the point of possible self-destruction, and, if we have someone's back, we'll likely put more energy into protecting them than defending ourselves. This brings me to the subject of boundaries. Water signs are more sensitive than most, and this is a tremendous gift, but we need to shore up our psychic defenses on the regular, and also understand when we might need grounding. Otherwise it can start to feel like it isn't a gift at all. Psychic self-defense is vital for everyone, not least because Scorpio knows that if our own minds are capable of all manner of things—both good and bad—other people's are as well. We don't want to stoke our characteristic paranoia; rather, we want to liberate ourselves to live as freely as we can, safe in the knowledge that we have strong boundaries that are reinforced lovingly—not fearfully—every day.

Energy Protection and the Auric Egg

We want to strengthen our boundaries to physically *and* energetically protect. We also want to ensure that we are aware of any tendency to self-sabotage, never mind outside influences causing us trouble. Finally, we want to ensure that our boundaries aren't such that they are blocking out that which is to our benefit.

A classic energy protection technique is the auric egg of light. Sit down quietly, call in your guides and the white light of the divine, and imagine yourself enclosed inside a bright, glowing ovoid of powerfully protective light, through which nothing negative can penetrate. Imagine the inside of the egg being filled with light that uplifts and heals, if you wish, but definitely conjure up the vision of an egg that is diamond-hard from the outside but you may emerge from whenever you wish.

I add the caveat that "this light repels and blocks anything that is not for my good, but easily magnetizes and admits the blessings that are my birthright," or something along those lines. You could also add in a line that stipulates that within this glowing dome of light "my highest and best qualities are strengthened and amplified," or "my mind, body, and spirit receive the divine rest and healing they need." Visualize the warm, glowing, golden-white light, radiating and dazzling. Tailor it depending on your needs—and how much time you have! The more you get into the habit of doing this—and I do recommend making this a daily practice (if not more frequently)—the quicker and more automatically you can slot that shield into place.

Meditating on the Archetypes

We're going to head into our caves for some quality time with ourselves. Scorpio understands more than most the power of silence and the dark and our fundamental need for it. However, sometimes our paranoid mindset can set us to overthinking when we create that kind of space for ourselves, so I'm going to suggest a visualization that will occupy that super-active brain of yours and connect you with the healing animal archetypes of the Scorpio star sign: the snake, the scorpion, the phoenix, the eagle, and the dove.

It's important to remember that the snake, although many feel repelled by it, is a symbol of healing and transformation, just like the phoenix. All the creatures associated with Scorpio can inspire our ascension and spiritual evolution when we give them our sincere focus. These archetypes are gifts for the Scorpio alone—no other sign has this family of animal helpers to draw upon.

When we consider the creatures in sequence—snake, scorpion, phoenix, eagle, and dove—something obvious stands out: they symbolically go from slithering on the ground, to the scorpion on its scuttling feet; the phoenix rising before bursting into flames, and then the eagle soaring with effortless power. Finally, the symbol of the eagle transforms into the dove, ascending lightly into the heavens, the ultimate image of grace, beauty, and peace. By using these archetypes, we can transmute shadow aspects, recognizing and releasing them, and ascending into the light.

Light a candle and go into a meditative state, and as you do so, imagine yourself as each of the archetypes in turn, shedding skins and old exoskeletons, molting away that which no longer serves, ascending, blazing, and regenerating before soaring into the sky with power and grace, positively changed. When you have completed this simple but profound visualization, sit quietly with a cup of tea and something to eat to ground yourself, and write down your thoughts. You have done some deep and powerful work. But then, you're a Scorpio witch—what else is new?

The Magic of the Underworld Ritual

Wendy Rule

Scorpio invites us to journey deep. Its fixed, watery nature beckons us to hold strong as we dig down through the layers of our deepest feelings and most secret selves. It calls us to transform, to shed the old skin and allow a new Self to emerge. For a Scorpio, this is true healing and self-care. Just as water on the surface of Earth will seep through layers of soil and stone to gather in cold, crystal-clear pools in the depths of caves, so too, when we allow space for the energy of Scorpio to lead us deep into the underworld, we gain access to our own magical pools of wisdom.

But this journey is often challenging. We must be brave enough to face our own shadow selves, to dig through layers of shame, or guilt, or depression, or grief. Thankfully, the Crone aspect of the Goddess is there to guide us. She guards the threshold from the Above to the Below, demanding of us our integrity, our truth, and our courage before she will grant us access to the gifts that lie below the surface.

Although the Sun only spends one twelfth of the year in Scorpio, we can honor the magic of the underworld every month when the Moon is dark. By turning inward, to stillness and self-reflection, every dark Moon becomes a powerful opportunity for divination, healing, and Self transformation.

You will need:
- ✦ A light-colored or clear bowl of water
- ✦ A candle
- ✦ A bottle of ink, food coloring, or liquid chlorophyll (my favorite choice!)
- ✦ Burn some myrrh resin or any incense you have on hand

Instructions:

In your private ritual space, gather these together. Turn the lights down low, light your candle, and spend a moment centering yourself before your altar. Now close your eyes and imagine you are deep below the surface of Earth, in a beautiful cave. It is peaceful and quiet, and you can sense the power in the rocks surrounding you. Take your time. Imagine the details. Water dripping. Smell of Earth. Really feel yourself here. Now open your eyes and recite this poem:

> *Through soil and stone*
> *Through fossil and bone*
> *I come here alone*
> *To honor the Crone*
> *The veils are thin*
> *And now I begin*
> *To open my mind*
> *To the wisdom within*

Think of a question or focus to ask the Crone. Place a few drops of the ink into the bowl of water, and watch as the patterns swirl, entering into trance as you gaze into the water. Observe your feelings, your thoughts, and the sensations in your body. Trust any insights that come through. Trust your own deep wisdom and know that the Crone speaks through you. Hold your focus for as long as possible. When you are ready, journal about your experience.

By holding space like this for the Crone each month, you will learn to navigate through times of darkness and harness the magic of the underworld.

DON'T BLAME IT ON YOUR SUN SIGN

Zoë Howe

Scorpio, so often proclaimed the most dangerous sign of the Zodiac (and to that I say thanks for noticing), is used to reading about our nefarious traits; astrologers are more sensitive these days in how they approach the subject of the Scorpio character, but some will remember books that painted us as positively villainous. The problem is, these descriptions can become a self-fulfilling prophecy, or lead one to sit back in resignation and say, "That's just me, I guess." We can even become defensive of the sides of Scorpio that others think are nasty and hold on to them rather tightly as we flip the bird at the rest of the world. Perhaps we're even relieved to have something to blame bad behavior on. But witches know about personal responsibility, and we also know we can effect changes if we want to. This chapter is going to look at the tricky traits and how we can grow through them.

Do remember that we are not just our Sun sign—we have a whole chart filled with different influences. You can easily work out at least your rising sign and Moon sign if you have your date, place, and time of birth on hand. This alone will give you a more detailed understanding of the planetary influences at play and will deepen your self-knowledge.

This Scorpio *Won't* Self-Destruct in Ten Seconds

In magical life, symbolism is all. We take on a lot of astrological traits when we associate ourselves closely with the symbol our sign represents: in our case, the scorpion. The characteristics of this lethal arachnid might not be particularly dominant in our own personalities at first, but we express all sorts of feelings every day, so when one seems typical of Scorpio, we, as pattern-loving humans, spot the link and subconsciously own it. But what happens if some of the supposed traits and behaviors we have been identifying with have actually been *misinterpreted?* It's time to update our settings. The following *may* blow your mind.

One of the most damaging assumptions about Scorpio is that we are self-destructive, self-sabotaging, our own worst enemy, and prone to wanting to check out when overwhelmed; this presumably originates from the "suicide" the scorpion commits when surrounded by fire. A lot of us genuinely *do* feel these things, but when you're constantly told you're more likely than anyone else to feel them, this can be potentially dangerous. However, in terms of Scorpionic behavior, it's also *not accurate*.

For one thing, it is arguably unlikely that a creature has the self-awareness to decide to end its own life. The movements a scorpion makes when surrounded by fire may *appear* to show that it is trying to sting itself, but what is happening is this: it is unable to regulate its body temperature due to the fire, and this causes the scorpion to experience spasms and convulsions.[4] It would be almost impossible for the sting to penetrate the exoskeleton—and apparently scorpions are immune to their own venom anyway. Maybe we can put that "self-destruct" cliché to bed, and move on from it, reflecting the scorpion archetype in a new, more resilient way. Yes, many of us do experience unhelpful thoughts and display unhelpful behaviors, but, to paraphrase the title of this chapter, *you can't necessarily blame it on your Sun sign*. We, Scorpio, can do or be anything we choose. We can regenerate, we can heal ourselves, we can rise like the phoenix. Let us plunge our stingers into these limiting assumptions and be our own best friends, not our own worst enemies.

One of the most magical things about the scorpion— something they *don't* ever mention—is that their exoskeletons contain fluorescent chemicals, which means they *glow*

---

4. Learn more at https://metode.org/metodes-whys-and-wherefores /why-do-scorpions-commit-suicide-when-surrounded-by-fire.html.

under ultraviolet light, or moonlight. We are lucky to be associated with these breathtaking creatures, creatures with capacities for beauty and illumination far beyond what we had previously been told. Own *those* scorpionic traits, and call on that glowing exoskeleton when you need it. Cast aside images of getting trapped, and stinging yourself to make the fear stop. Scorpio doesn't do that. Scorpio shines. Scorpio *rises*.

Befriending Our Sexual Power

We've talked about making friends with our stings earlier in the book (Recharging and Self-Care, page 159). But some of us could do with connecting more meaningfully with that famous Scorpio sexuality. Society can try to squash our sexuality, especially in young women who might be powerfully sexy before they even realize it. This squashing can be intended to protect, but the blunt act of repressing it can leave us damaged and confused. We need to heal our sexuality to bring it back to its natural power, unimpeded by anyone else's agenda.

Sexual energy is potent, so we want to understand it to use it in our magical practice and to feel natural about it. Healthy sexuality is not dangerous. We may have been told it is by a victim-blaming culture, but our sexuality is an important part of us, a gift that deserves to be loved, integrated, and healed if necessary. Journaling about this, using shadow or energy work, can illuminate what needs to be healed. For the moment, don't worry about the *how*; just check in with how you are doing in this regard and set the healing wheels in motion.

Release Those Pincers

Scorpio has a gift for feeling so intensely furious about a subject, situation, or circumstance, we practically preserve it from the moment we give it our attention, because if we let it go, we may have "allowed" an injustice to slip through. But it is usually ourselves we end up punishing, holding ourselves chained to a moment in time while the other person has moved on. This can muddy our magic, and our lives, if we aren't careful.

I have noticed that when I deliberately rebel against that tendency and refuse to react or make a memorandum of the situation, it often flies away and leaves little to no dent on me. This depends on the situation of course, but I'm sure you can think of examples that correlate, situations that were irritating but that—admit it—have become more poisonous in your amplification of them, festering in your psyche like a lump of old cheese. *You don't have to do this* just because we are told this is a Scorpio thing.

We are the masters of our own destiny, and, as all witches know, free will is all. Use it, and don't resign yourself to expressing traits of your sign that end up only damaging you. Draw on your self-discipline. You can hang on to something of ultimately little import with those pincers and be tense and miserable, or you can scuttle into a moonbeam and glow and dance with your lover, before calling up your old pal Stingy and paralyzing something nice to eat.

Single-Minded Scorpio

Scorpio is frequently defined by extremes, and, let's face it, extremes sound rather more exciting than bland, beige, vanilla qualities that hover somewhere in the middle. We find ourselves embodying those extremes in different ways, and, as discussed earlier, they can lead to unhealthy tendencies to work and play too hard, invariably leading to burnout. However, many of us find constructive ways of working with the extreme nature of Scorpio that we're so often told about.

For example, we generally prefer to concentrate intently on one thing at once rather than multitask, and in some contexts this is an excellent trait to have; we are not easily distracted, and we give people, situations, Netflix, our undivided attention. The flipside of this can be that we are so blinkered in our focus that some things escape our attention.

This fast-moving world demands that we have several plates spinning. If we can't do this, we judge ourselves— harshly, if you're a Scorpio. But while accepting that it's not always possible to dedicate ourselves to one thing at a time, we can allow ourselves to do *exactly* this if we believe certain distractions are at odds with our hearts, souls, or values. We don't always have the luxury to choose, but sometimes we do, and this is where we have to be discerning. We don't *have* to scroll social media if we feel that it exposes us to scenarios that disturb our peace, for example. If that means taking a break from it and looking antisocial or uninvolved, so be it. You're a mysterious, remote Scorpio. People expect it.

Women in particular feel that they have to take on everything, and in this era it has been made easier than ever to do lots of things at the same time, fast, and visibly so. This attitude is infectious and can seep into all areas of our lives, and that includes spirituality and magic. Make like your element of water and try to be flexible, allowing yourself to be guided into areas that are right for you—and that involves keeping those paths of intuition clear (no distractions). Don't, on the other hand, fall into the trap of getting bamboozled by the dizzying array of spells, meditations, lectures, and books that are out there, all apparently vying for your attention and all equal, supposedly, in importance. They're not. Put some on ice and put some in the fire while concentrating on what you need to do *now*, if that's how your Scorpio energy manifests.

Co Easy on Yourself, and Celebrate the Wins

We're serious, we're difficult, we're critical. That's what we're told, and it's exhausting, not least because it's true. But as always, we have a choice and we don't have to embody *any* trait that doesn't work for us just because we are so attached to being a Scorpio with everything that means. We are all or nothing, but we could maybe do with getting better at tailoring and customizing the Scorpio experience so we can live some of the more helpful traits in a way that empowers our lives.

One thing I'd like to say is, don't make everything harder than it needs to be. Some things—yes, like magic—come easily to you, but generally we have such a level of self-doubt that we believe it can't be proper or we aren't doing it right if it flows too naturally. But maybe we are. Accept it rather than tripping yourself up because you don't trust what comes easily. Acknowledge your gifts with appreciation.

Sometimes it feels as if we are in competition with ourselves, only as good as our last mistake, which we go over and over in our minds. I know we find it hard to trust, we get paranoid and sometimes nothing will reassure us, but let's write down every time we know that we *do* get it right, every time someone pours some sugar on us (but don't rely solely on external validation to know you are succeeding). There will be more examples than you anticipated, and acknowledging them will build self-trust. Believe them, trust them, take them, and celebrate them, because they are real.

Heart Unbinding Spell

Dayan Skipper-Martinez

This spell came to me from the chthonic gods of the underworld. It is meant to dredge up strong feelings and memories. This is sympathetic magic and it can be paired with journaling during the spell. In true Scorpio fashion, lean into your deep emotions and the sensual aspects of the process.

The ritual is done over a period of two weeks. It is best to start the first rite on a full Moon, to connect with healing energies and illuminate the deep recesses of the soul. If so, the final rite will take place on the cleansing new Moon.

You will need:

+ A very red apple
+ Four feet of golden cotton thread
+ Honey
+ Small bowl (to hold the apple)
+ Large bowl to fill with water

Instructions:

On the first Moon, begin by creating sacred space; make sure it is quiet and private. Enter a meditative mindset and connect with any emotional turmoil you feel. Pick up the golden thread in one hand and the red apple in the other hand.

Slowly begin to wrap the thread around the apple. Let your pace and direction follow your emotions. Speak the names dredged up, the haunting memories, your insecurities, and challenges. Feel each of them deeply and bind them into the thread and the apple.

Once this is done, set the gold-bound apple into the bowl. Pour the honey over the apple, slowly. The honey will "seal up" what you've created and work its healing magic. Set it away somewhere you can see and notice daily.

On the second Moon, create your sacred space as before. Enter a meditative mindset and focus on the bound apple and remember all it represents:

+ The apple is your heart, bound.
+ The golden cotton thread is what binds and hurts you.
+ The honey is the gentle healing we receive.

Hold the apple and connect with it, the thread, and the symbols they represent. Find the end of the thread and begin to pull it loose. Name each of the things bound, now coming free. Feel the relief of it; breathe into it deeply. Pause as needed, but feel each moment as you get lighter and freer. Give yourself permission to release emotions as they arise.

Once unbound, wash the apple in the bowl with water. Sing or chant or laugh to celebrate this release. Once finished, discard the apple into a pond or river and cut up and bury the thread. As you do, say aloud,

Let this heart be free,
Let its burdens fall.
Wisdom learned and bound,
Power gained in gold.

Depart that place without looking back and keep your witch work silent.

POSTCARD FROM A SCORPIO WITCH

Lisa Jade

When Ivo asked me to contribute to this compilation, it was immediately clear to me that I would contribute on the almost comedic-tragic nature of how a Scorpio Sun sign gets into the near-abyss depths of spiritual practice. In this essay, I hope you'll find some of your own truths reflected, and greater understanding of the faceted depth of the Scorpio. To connect with the energy of a zodiacal constellation, or any celestial event, that energy must be translated to us via planetary bodies. In this case, that planetary body is the Sun. As the Sun moves through the constellations that create Scorpio in the sky, it distributes the qualities of depth seeking and intensity within those born under this sign.

For me and many Sun sign Scorpios, we are anything but surface-level conversationalists. As a wonderful teacher once described, seeking the depths can be a bit like peering into the abyss described in the Kabbalistic Tree of Life. It is a look into unfathomable depths of knowledge, there to perhaps be explored, but with the risk that one can be lost within them. What I am learning as a Scorpio in her late thirties is that in order to enjoy getting into the depths, we need to resurface. When Scorpio does this process, we can soar to the highest heights as the mythological phoenix also associated with the sign. It is the process of regeneration and transformation, driven by the instinctual way in which we move through spiritual progress.

In witchcraft, this means we are meant to do some deep dives into spiritual work, meditation, journeying (especially into cave imagery), ancestral healing. You know, the light stuff. This is a gift we have! Scorpios love exploring the shadow realm, the ecstatic, the pulsating rhythm of the Earth herself. The way in which we avoid drowning is in the resurfacing, like a scuba diver might between dives. As we get into the depth of our craft, resurfacing (having time to process and just be) helps us fully integrate the teaching obtained on each deep dive. Should we become obsessive about each dive and limit the time in an integrative process, we do ourselves a disservice. If we do not integrate the wisdom afforded to us, we can't build a practice. That is the downfall of Scorpio in my opinion. We begin to think we have dived so deep that we are all-knowing. We may be stuck with a snorkel in the shallow end of our Craft.

My encouragement is to put effort into a daily practice and follow some type of rhythm that allows space for both depth of practice and breathing. In my personal practice, I work with the planetary cycles of retrograding and turning direct as that guide to processing. You might use the phases of the Moon or the sabbats and their changing tides of a lighter half of the year into a darker half. In whatever manner you work your witchery, fellow Scorpio, know this: you can only descend into the depths as far as you rise up and transform.

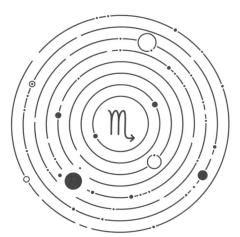

• SPIRIT OF SCORPIO GUIDANCE RITUAL •

Ivo Dominguez, Jr.

The signs are more than useful constructs in astrology or categories for describing temperaments, they are also powerful and complicated spiritual entities. So, what is meant when we say that a sign is a spirit? I often describe the signs of the zodiac as the twelve forms of human wisdom and folly. The signs are twelve styles of human consciousness, which also means that the signs are well-developed group minds and egregores. Think on the myriad of people over thousands of years who have poured energy into the constructs of the signs through intentional visualization and study. Moreover, the lived experience of each person as one of the signs is deposited into the group minds and egregores of their sign. Every Scorpio who has ever lived or is living contributes to the spirit of Scorpio.

The signs have a composite nature that allows them to exist in many forms on multiple planes of reality at once. In addition to the human contribution to their existence, the spirits of the signs are made from inputs from all living beings in our world whether they are made of dense matter or spiritual substances. These vast and ancient thoughtforms that became group minds and then egregores are also vessels that can be used by divine beings to communicate with humans as well. The spirits of the signs can manifest themselves as small as a sprite or larger than the Earth. The shape and the magnitude of the spirit of Scorpio emerging before you will depend on who you are and how and why you call upon them.

Purpose and Use

This ritual will make it possible to commune with the spirit of Scorpio. The form that the spirit will take will be different each time you perform the ritual. What appears will be determined by what you are looking for and your state of mind and soul. The process for preparing yourself for the ritual will do you good as well. Aligning yourself with the source and core of your energy is a useful practice in and of itself. Exploring your circumstances, motivations, and intentions is a valuable experience whether or not you are performing this ritual.

If you have a practical problem you are trying to solve or an obstacle that must be overcome, the spirit of Scorpio may have useful advice. If you are trying to better understand who you are and what you are striving to accomplish, then the spirit of Scorpio can be your mentor. Should you have a need to recharge yourself or flush out stale energy, you can use this ritual to reconnect with a strong clear current of power that is compatible with your core. This energy can be used for magickal empowerment, physical vitality, or healing, or redirected for spell work. If you are charging objects or magickal implements with Scorpio energy, this ritual can be used for this purpose as well.

Timing for the Ritual

The prevailing astrological conditions have an impact on how you experience a ritual, the type and amount of power available, and the outcomes of the work. If you decide you want to go deeper in your studies of astrology, you'll find many techniques to pick the best day and time for your ritual. Thankfully, the ritual to meet the spirit of your sign does not require exact timing or perfect astrological conditions. This ritual depends on your inner connection to your Sun sign, so it is not as reliant on the external celestial conditions as some other rituals. Each of us has worlds within ourselves that include inner landscapes and inner skies. Your birth chart, and the sky that it depicts, shines brightest within you. Although not required, you can improve the effectiveness of this ritual if you use any of the following simple guidelines for favorable times:

+ When the Moon or the Sun is in Scorpio.
+ When Mars is in Scorpio or Capricorn where it is exalted.
+ On Tuesday, the day of Mars, and even better at dawn, which is its planetary hour.
+ When the Sun is in or near the fifteenth degree of Scorpio, which is a few days after Samhain in the northern hemisphere and Beltane in the southern hemisphere.

Materials and Setup

The following is a description of the physical objects that will make it easier to perform this ritual. Don't worry if you don't have all of them; in a pinch, you need no props. However, the physical objects will help anchor the energy and your mental focus.

You will need:

- ✦ A printout of your birth chart
- ✦ A table to serve as an altar
- ✦ A chair if you want to sit during the ritual
- ✦ A small bowl of water with a few drops of vinegar, wine, or citrus juice to represent the element of water
- ✦ An assortment of items for the altar that correspond to Scorpio or Pluto or Mars (obsidian, a bone, a hat pin or some other proxy for a stinger, black pansy flowers, or a piece of an aloe plant)
- ✦ A pad and a pen or chalk and a small blackboard or something else you can use to draw a glyph

Before beginning the ritual, you may wish to copy the ritual invocations onto paper or bookmark this chapter and bring the book into the ritual. I find that the process of writing out the invocation, whether handwritten or typed, helps forge a better connection with the words and their meaning. If possible, put the altar table in the center of your space, and if not, then as close to due east as you can manage. Place the bowl with the water on the altar and hold your hand over it. Send warming energy from your hand to the water. Put your birth chart on the altar to one side of the bowl and arrange the items you have selected to anchor the Scorpio and planetary energy around it. To the other side of the bowl, place the pad and pen. Make sure you turn off your phone, close the door, close the curtains, or do whatever else is needed to prevent distractions.

Ritual to Meet the Spirit of Your Sign

You may stand or be seated—whichever is the most comfortable for you. Begin by focusing on your breathing. When you pay attention to the process of breathing, you become more aware of your body, the flow of your life energy, and the balance between conscious and unconscious actions. After you have done so for about a minute, it is time to shift into fourfold breathing. This consists of four phases: inhaling, lungs full, exhaling, and lungs empty. You count to keep time so that each of the four phases is of equal duration. Try a count of four or five in your first efforts. Depending on your lungs and how fast you count, you will need to adjust the number higher or lower. When you hold your breath, hold it with your belly muscles, not your throat. When you hold your breath in fourfold breathing, your throat should feel relaxed. Be gentle and careful with yourself if you have asthma, high blood pressure, are late in pregnancy, or have any other condition that may have an impact on your breathing and blood pressure. In general, if there are difficulties, they arise during the lungs full or empty phases because of clenching the throat or compressing the lungs. The empty and the full lungs should be held by the position of the diaphragm and the air passages left open. After one to three minutes of fourfold breathing, you can return to your normal breathing pattern.

Now close your eyes and move your center of consciousness down into the middle of your chest. Proceed with grounding and centering, dropping and opening, shifting into the alpha state, or whatever practice you use to reach the state of mind that supports ritual work. Then gaze deeply inside yourself and find yourself sitting on the ground in a garden under a velvety sky filled with stars. Take a breath and smell fresh air and sweet fragrances on the evening breeze. Let the beauty of the night awaken all the places and spaces within you that are of Scorpio. When you feel ready, open your eyes. Dip a finger into the bowl.

Zodiac Casting

If you are seated, stand if you are able and face the east. Slowly read this invocation aloud, putting some energy into your words. As you read it, slowly turn counterclockwise so that you come full circle when you reach the last line. Another option is to hold your hand over your head and trace the counterclockwise circle of the zodiac with your finger.

> *I call forth the twelve to join me in this rite.*
> *I call forth Aries and the power of courage.*
> *I call forth Taurus and the power of stability.*
> *I call forth Gemini and the power of versatility.*
> *I call forth Cancer and the power of protection.*
> *I call forth Leo and the power of the will.*
> *I call forth Virgo and the power of discernment.*
> *I call forth Libra and the power of harmony.*
> *I call forth Scorpio and the power of renewal.*
> *I call forth Sagittarius and the power of vision.*
> *I call forth Capricorn and the power of*
>   *responsibility.*
> *I call forth Aquarius and the power of innovation.*
> *I call forth Pisces and the power of compassion.*
> *The power of the twelve is here.*
> *Blessed be!*

Take a few deep breaths and gaze at the bowl of water. Become aware of the changes in the atmosphere around you and the presence of the twelve signs.

Altar Work

Pick up the printout of your birth chart and look at your chart. Touch each of the twelve houses with your finger and push energy into them. You are energizing and awakening your birth chart to act as a focal point of power on the altar. Put your chart back on the altar when it feels ready to you. Then take the pad and pen and write the glyph for Scorpio again and again. The glyphs can be different sizes, they can overlap; you can make any pattern with them you like so long as you pour energy into the ink as you write. Scribing the glyph is an action that helps draw the interest of the spirit of Scorpio. Periodically look at the water in the bowl as you continue scribing the glyph. When you feel sensations in your body such as electric tingles, warmth, shivers, or something that you associate with the approach of a spirit, it is time to move on to the next step. If these are new experiences for you, just follow your instincts. Put away the pen and paper and pick up the sheet with the invocation of Scorpio.

Invoking Scorpio

Before beginning to read this invocation, get in touch with your feelings. Think on what you hope to accomplish in this ritual and why it matters to you. Then speak these lines slowly and with conviction.

> Scorpio, hear me, for I am born of the primeval depths of fixed water.
> Scorpio, see me, for the Scorpio Sun shines upon me.
> Scorpio, know me as a member of your family and your company.
> Scorpio, know me as your student and your protégé.
> Scorpio, know me as a conduit for your power.
> Scorpio, know me as a wielder of your magick.
> I am of you, and you are of me.
> I am of you, and you are of me.
> I am of you, and you are of me.
> Scorpio is here within and without.
> Blessed be!

Your Requests

Now look inward for several deep breaths, and silently or aloud welcome the spirit of Scorpio. Dip a finger into the bowl of water and draw it out. Close your eyes and ask for any guidance that would be beneficial for you and listen. It may take some time before anything comes through, so be patient. I find it valuable to receive guidance before making a request so that I can refine or modify intentions and outcomes. Consider the meaning of whatever impressions or guidance you received and reaffirm your intentions and desired outcomes for this ritual.

It is more effective to use multiple modes of communication to make your request. Speak silently or aloud the words that describe your need and how it could be solved. Visualize the same message but without the words and project the images on your mind's screen. Then put all your attention on your feelings and your bodily sensations that have been stirred up by contemplating your appeal to the spirit of Scorpio. Once again wait and use all your physical and psychic senses to perceive what is given. At this point in the ritual if there are objects to be charged, touch them or focus your gaze on them.

Offer Gratitude

You may be certain or uncertain about the success of the ritual or the time frame for the outcomes to become clear. Regardless of that, it is a good practice to offer thanks and gratitude to the spirit of Scorpio for being present. Also, thank yourself for doing your part of the work. The state of heart and mind that comes with thanks and gratitude makes it easier for the work to become manifest. Thanks and gratitude also act as a buffer against the unintended consequences that can be put into motion by rituals.

Release the Ritual

If you are seated, stand if you are able and face the east. Slowly turn clockwise until you come full circle while repeating the following or something similar.

> *Return, return oh turning wheel to your*
> *starry home.*
> *Farewell, farewell oh soul-searching Scorpio*
> *until we speak again.*

Another option while saying these words is to hold your hand over your head and trace a clockwise circle of the zodiac with your finger. When you are done, snuff out the candle on the altar and say,

It is done. It is done. It is done.

Afterward

I encourage you to write down your thoughts and observations of what you experienced in the ritual. Do this while it is still fresh in mind before the details begin to blur. The information will become more useful over time as you work more with the spirit of Scorpio. It will also let you evaluate the outcomes of your workings and improve your process in future workings. This note-taking or journaling will also help you dial in any changes or refinements to this ritual for future use. Contingent on the guidance you received or the outcomes you desire, you may want to add reminders to your calendar.

More Options

These are some modifications to this ritual that you may wish to try:

+ Put together or purchase Scorpio incense to burn during the ritual. A Scorpio oil to anoint yourself or add to the water is another possibility. I'm providing one of my oil recipes as a possibility.

+ Set up a richer and deeper altar. In addition to adding more objects that resonate to the energy of Scorpio or Pluto, consecrate each object before the ritual. You may also want to place an altar cloth on the table that suggests Scorpio, Pluto, or the element of water.

+ Creating a sigil to concentrate the essence of what you are working toward would be a good addition to the altar.

+ Consider adding chanting, free-form toning, or movement to raise energy for the altar work and/or for invoking Scorpio.

If you feel inspired, you can write your own invocations for calling the zodiac and/or invoking Scorpio. This is a great way to deepen your understanding of the signs and to personalize your ritual.

Rituals have greater meaning and effectiveness when you personalize them and make them your own.

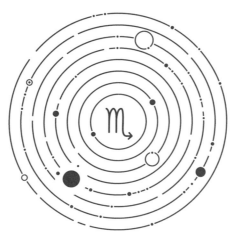

SCORPIO ANOINTING OIL RECIPE

* * *

Ivo Dominguez, Jr.

This oil is used for charging and consecrating candles, crystals, and other objects you use in your practice. This oil makes it easier for an object to be imbued with Scorpio energy. It also primes and tunes the objects so that your will and power as a Scorpio witch flow more easily into them. Do not apply the oil to your skin unless you have done an allergy test first.

Ingredients:

+ Carrier oil—1 ounce
+ Pine—6 drops
+ Labdanum—6 drops
+ Palmarosa—4 drops
+ Myrrh—4 drops
+ Eucalyptus—2 drops

Pour one ounce of a carrier oil into a small bottle or vial. The preferred carrier oils are almond oil or fractionated coconut oil. Other carrier oils can be used. If you use olive oil, the blend will have a shorter shelf life. Ideally, use essential oils, but fragrance oils can be used as substitutes. Add the drops of the essential oils into the carrier. Once they are all added, cap the bottle tightly, and shake the bottle several times. Hold the bottle in your hands, take a breath, and pour energy into the oil. Visualize crimson energy or repeat the word *Scorpio* or raise energy in your preferred manner. Continue doing so until the oil feels warm, seems to glow, or you sense that it is charged.

Label the bottle and store the oil in a cool, dark place. Consider keeping a little bit of each previous batch of oil to add to the new batch. This helps build the strength and continuity of the energy and intentions you have placed in the oil. Over time, that link makes your oils more powerful.

• BETTER EVERY DAY: THE WAY FORWARD •

Zoë Howe

Scorpio witch, we know we have uncompromising qualities. Hopefully now we have a better idea as to how we can make those qualities work for us, channeling them into forming good magical habits that make our life better and our magic stronger. You will have come across many thoughts and ideas throughout this book, and I'm going to send you off with a few more to mull over, and invite into your life, if you wish, to keep that power pure, potent, and regenerative.

Transform, Transmute, and Rise with the Violet Flame

Scorpio relates easily to the idea of burning things down and blazing through problems, and so the image of the violet flame of transmutation is a great one to call upon in everyday life. For anything—big or small—and at any time. For me it relates to the transformative phoenix energy that helps us shift through obstacles effortlessly.

You may well already be very familiar with the violet flame, but for those who are not, the concept is that of a living, sacred flame of such high frequency that it can transmute and transform anything into its highest potential and into useful, positive energy. It is associated with many ascended masters, but perhaps most famously we hear it being connected with Archangel Zadkiel, the ascended master St. Germain, and the qualities of mercy, compassion, and joy.

There are countless videos and reams of literature out there offering guidance in calling on the violet flame. What I love about this practice is that, once you are familiar with it, it is easy to visualize, and placing situations, things, yourself, even the entire globe into the violet fire feels like a healthy way of changing state and powerfully burning through that which no longer serves.

We Scorpios are a bit too good at holding on to things (like grudges), but try the following exercise, dissolve what needs dissolving in the ray of violet fire, and see how you feel afterward. Call in your spirit team or the white light of the divine to cloak and ground you in perfect protection before you begin.

1. Imagine something you wish to let go of—like a grudge—as whole and solid, and see yourself placing it into this flame.
2. Imagine walking into it yourself, sitting in it, bathing in it—the flame never scorches you; it is cool and comfortable.
3. Request and know that the energy you are handing over to this exquisite purple fire is being transmuted easily and instantly into pure love.
4. Visualize the healing violet light filling the spaces where your psychic wounds used to be, filling any vacuum and sealing it.
5. Come back into your body, take a few grounding breaths, wriggle hands and feet. You are ready to come back into the rest of your day. Don't be surprised if you notice violet around you a lot more, on walks, in the form of spirit lights (pinpricks of colored light you perceive in the air), or in your dreams.

Drawing on the Wisdom of Father Scorpio

I was, for a while, Scorpio-suspicious of ceremonial magic. I accept this as rather narrow-minded now, but I admit that I probably felt intimidated by it, perceived that maybe it was patriarchal, and perhaps that it looked down on witches like myself. While some of the above is certainly true in some cases, I was wrong to dismiss "high magic" and its place in my life outright. Happy to admit it. Holding my pincers up here. Part of my own Scorpio journey has been working on decalcifying some of my more hardened astrological traits—suspicion, rigidity—and be more open to other ways of doing things.

A good friend mentioned the name of Israel Regardie, a former member of the Hermetic Order of the Golden Dawn. I looked him up and felt magnetized to his book *The Art of True Healing: The Unlimited Power of Prayer and Visualization* (New World Library, 2013), which contains his Middle Pillar meditation, connecting to the middle pillar of the Kabbalistic Tree of Life. I tried it once and felt instant healing in my hand, in which I had been experiencing painful circulation issues. Warmth rushed into the affected area, and remained there. I was amazed, and vowed to commit to the Middle Pillar meditation, always with gratitude in my heart for Israel Regardie.

There isn't space here to do more than point you in the direction of his work, but one of the reasons I wanted to mention

Israel Regardie is because he himself was, if not a Scorpio witch, certainly a Scorpio occultist known as, among other names, Father Scorpio. Born on November 17, evidently Regardie's Sun sign meant a lot to him, so he seemed the perfect person to draw on for this book. Regardie shared wisdom and magical knowledge he knew would help people; admittedly, this was at odds with the secretive Scorpio nature (and didn't always go down well), although it is very much in line with Scorpio's desire to bring healing.

It is worth noting that Regardie recommended learning how to use the Lesser Banishing Ritual of the Pentagram and using it frequently for some months before attempting the Middle Pillar exercise. Occultists familiar with the Kabbalah and the practices of the Golden Dawn will already know these rituals. For those of you who don't, I encourage you to learn about them if you feel called to. Because they work.

Abracadabra Spell

Charms such as the Abracadabra spell have been used for centuries to both attract as well as banish—and as we work on our personal development every day (did I mention shadow work?), the typical Scorpio will likely want to do both, considering what needs to go before filling the space with something more desirable. This is healthy and smart: nature abhors a vacuum, so take control over what fills it. *Abracadabra* can be loosely translated as "I create what I speak," but it also relates to the Aramaic phrase *abhadda kedabhra* (disappear like this word).[5] Have the meaning that is most appropriate for your needs in mind as you work the charm.

First, we are going to "disappear" something.

You will need:

+ Pen and two pieces of paper
+ Matches or lighter and firesafe container
+ Locket or pot for planting (optional)

5. Joshua Hehe, "Abracadabra: The Famous Word of Power," *Medium*, December 23, 2019, https://joshuashawnmichael hehe.medium.com/abracadabra-a99be321d7f9.

Instructions:

On the dark Moon, take a pen and paper and consider what you would like to banish. Write your intention on one side, and then flip it over and, as you focus on your intention and the charm *disappear like this word*, write down the word *Abracadabra*. Then, directly underneath, write it again but with the last letter missing. Then repeat with the last two letters missing and so on until you get to the single *A* at the bottom. The letters should look like an inverted pyramid—a potent symbol in itself for manifestation and magic.

ABRACADABRA

ABRACADABR

ABRACADAB

ABRACADA

ABRACAD

ABRACA

ABRAC

ABRA

ABR

AB

A

Once the Moon moves from dark into new, consider what you would like to attract and work the charm in reverse, writing your wish on one side of the paper, then, on the reverse, starting with the single *A* of *Abracadabra*, and writing it in the pyramid shape, widening out to the full word at the bottom, thinking of your intention and the words *I create what I speak.* It should look like this:

A
AB
ABR
ABRA
ABRAC
ABRACA
ABRACAD
ABRACADA
ABRACADAB
ABRACADABR
ABRACADABRA

Now you have created the new charm, it is time to release the previous day's banishment—burning the paper (safely) and depositing the ashes at a crossroads will do nicely. As for the drawing charm, you could wear it in a locket until your desire manifests, burn it to release your intention into the invisible realm, or roll it into a scroll and tuck it into a pot and plant a seed or bulb next to it. This is a common way of manifesting, and a reassuring one; as we physically see our plant emerge, we can visualize our goal coming into being too.

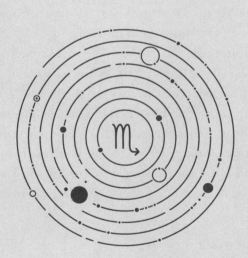

Scorpio Witch Affirmations

Thanks to our fixed nature, we find it easy to stick to exercises that involve repetition and habitual activities over periods of time when we know that the results are going to bring us what we want. This means that we have no issue maintaining regular practices using mantras and affirmations that others might lose patience with after five minutes.

I've conjured up some affirmations for the Scorpio witch that connect with our typical traits. Pick the ones that call to you at pertinent times. Read them aloud or silently in your head, or record them in your own voice (and feel free to add in any affirmations of your own if you are called to do so). Use them for at least twenty-one days in a row to create a habit and effect positive transformation.

Scorpio heals, Scorpio regenerates, and Scorpio communicates—on multiple levels. When we turn our healing regenerative focus onto ourselves—communicating with our bodies, minds, and souls—we build a foundation that allows us to do great work for others. It has been a pure privilege to communicate with my fellow Scorpio witches through these pages, and I offer the following to you with love. I wish you ease, grace, balance, and joy in your Scorpio witchery, and your life.

I trust myself
It is safe to be powerful
I use my power for my highest good, and the good of all

I am strong and empowered

I am a force for positive transformation

I am fearless

I make friends with myself

I am friends with my sting, which guards and protects

I love and am thankful for my sting

I am in control of my sting; I am in control of my formidable power and strength

I am in control of my sexuality and express it in healthy, joyful ways; I revel in its positive power

I know who I am

Other people's judgments and fears have no effect on me

I am invincible

I glow and shine with unearthly beauty

I feel safe in the darkness

I embrace the light

I am psychically protected

I am safe and secure in every way

I am in tune with my intuition, and I trust my instincts

I am healthy in mind, body, and spirit, emotionally, sexually, and in every way

I am letting go of that which no longer serves my highest good with ease

I find it easy to release that which no longer serves

I let go of resentments and replace them with pure healing light

I release old wounds and fill the space with healing light and compassion

I allow myself to forgive myself and others for my own sake

I allow myself to move on and embrace my glittering future, unimpeded by the past

I am enough, and I know what to do

I am grateful for my knowledge and power, and thank my higher Self for guiding me on this magical path

I am always in touch with my higher Self, my spirit team, with the divine, and I allow myself to be divinely guided and inspired

I am always guided and inspired by divine wisdom and love

I always know I can hand over any situation to divine love for perfect solution

I move on from overthinking and paranoia, and I replace these with clarity, self-trust, and confidence

So mote it be, and so it is!

A Tarot Spell for Release

Rhonda Alin

In tarot, the Major Arcana Death card is aligned with Scorpio and is the center of this tarot spell for release. First, ask yourself what you need to release. Be as clear and precise as possible.

Take a tarot deck of your choice, focus on the issue, shuffle, and stack your cards. Use the three cards pulled in the spread to build your spell. Do not feel rushed; allow yourself time to prepare for the periods before, during, and after the work.

Turn over one card at a time until you locate the Death card.

The card prior to the Death card is card #1 and the energy that supports you or is your ally as you go through the work of release.

As you build your spell, identify correspondences to each card to use in your work. Include herbs, stones, songs, actions, a meal, or offerings that support the card's energy.

How does card #1 support the work of release? If it's cups, does it help wash away and provide healing? Swords, does it clarify, clear, and cut away what stands between you and change? Pentacles, does it help shift the ground beneath your feet or does it allow the Earth to open and remove what is an obstacle in your path? If it's wands, does it support the burning away of waste that doesn't support you or your goal? If it's another Major Arcana card, how does it partner with Death to lend its support?

The Death card (card #2) represents your commitment to embracing the release needed. Spend time in meditation on what it is that you are seeking to move beyond. Know that you, like Death, are an undeniable force and are moving through and away from a person, situation, or thing. Include a physical action in your spell to embody the internal commitment of what you are releasing. For example, using a staff, a stick, a sword, a line in the dirt, or a line written in chalk, stand on one side and, holding your Death card, focus on what you are releasing; speak it out loud and, once finished, step across the line, echoing the movement of Death as it moves forward, unstoppable.

The card that follows Death (card #3) is what awaits you now that you have committed to releasing what is no longer needed. What do you need to prepare for once you've made this release? What supports or challenges you in this shift?

Remember, releasing something leaves space in your world for something else to take its place. Know ahead of time what it is that you'd like to fill that space and, if nothing else, have a neutral or innocuous placeholder available until you are clear about what it is you really want.

Finally, celebrate your irrefutable Scorpionic power of walking in step with death, transition, change, and release!

CONCLUSION

Ivo Dominguez, Jr.

n o doubt, you are putting what you discovered in this book to use in your witchcraft. You may have a desire to learn more about how astrology and witchcraft fit together. One of the best ways to do this is to talk about it with other practitioners. Look for online discussions, and if there is a local metaphysical shop, check to see if they have classes or discussion groups. If you don't find what you need, consider creating a study group. Learning more about your own birth chart is also an excellent next step.

At some point, you may wish to call upon the services of an astrologer to give you a reading that is fine-tuned to your chart. There are services that provide not just charts but full chart readings that are generated by software. These are a decent tool and more economical than a professional astrologer, but they lack the finesse and intuition only a person can offer. Nonetheless, they can be a good starting point. If you do decide to hire an astrologer to do your chart, shop around to find someone attuned to your spiritual needs. You may decide to learn enough astrology to read your own chart, and that will serve you for many reasons. However, most practitioners of a divinatory art will seek out another practitioner rather than read for themselves in important matters. It is hard to see some things when you are too attached to the outcomes.

If you find your interest in astrology and its effect on a person's relationship to witchcraft has been stimulated by this book, you may wish to read the other books in this series. Additionally, if you have other witches you work with, you'll find that knowing more about how they approach their craft will make your collective efforts more productive. Understanding them better will also help reduce conflicts or misunderstandings. The ending of this book is really the beginning of an adventure. Go for it.

APPENDIX
SCORPIO CORRESPONDENCES

October 22/23–November 21/23

Symbol: ♏

Solar System: Mars, Pluto

Season: Autumn

Day: Tuesday

Runes: Eoh, Nyd

Element: Water

Colors: Black, Blue, Brown (Reddish), Crimson, Gray, Green, Maroon, Orange, Red

Energy: Yin

Chakras: Root, Sacral

Numbers: 8, 9

Tarot: Death, Swords

Trees: Ash, Blackthorn, Palm, Pine, Pomegranate

Herb and Garden: Anemone, Basil, Blackberry/ Bramble, Chrysanthemum, Dill, Gardenia,

Heather, Honeysuckle, Ivy, Lady's Mantle, Lily, Valerian, Violet

Miscellaneous Plants: Allspice, Clove, Cumin, Deer's Tongue, Galangal, Ginger, Horehound, Myrrh, Nettle, Patchouli, Reed, Saffron, Thistle, Vanilla

Gemstones and Minerals: Agate (Snakeskin), Alexandrite, Aquamarine, Beryl, Bloodstone, Carnelian, Citrine, Garnet (Red), Jasper (Red), Kunzite, Labradorite, Larimar, Malachite, Moonstone, Obsidian, Opal, Peridot, Quartz (Rutilated), Rhodochrosite, Ruby, Topaz, Tourmaline, Turquoise, Zircon

Metal: Copper, Iron, Steel

From the Sea: Coral (Black), Pearl

Goddesses: Ereshkigal, Hecate, Hel, Isis, Persephone

God: Anubis, Mars, Njord, Osiris, Pluto, Set

Angel: Gabriel

Animal: Dog, Panther, Wolf

Birds: Eagle, Hawk, Vulture

Reptile: Snake

Insect: Scorpion

Mythical: Phoenix

Issues, Intentions, and Powers: Authority, Change, Clairvoyance, Control, Creativity, Darkness, Death, Desire, Destruction, Determination, Discipline, Emotions, Energy, Healing, Introspection, Jealousy, Love, Loyalty, Lust, Magic (Sex), Otherworld/Underworld, Passion, Power, Psychic Ability, Rebirth/Renewal (General, Emotional), Revenge, Secrets, Senses, Sexuality, Spirituality, Success, Transformation, Trust (Distrust), Willpower

Excerpted with permission from *Llewellyn's Complete Book of Correspondences: A Comprehensive & Cross-Referenced Resource for Pagans & Wiccans* © 2013 by Sandra Kynes.

RESOURCES

Online

Astrodienst: Free birth charts and many resources.

+ https://www.astro.com/horoscope

Astrolabe: Free birth chart and software resources.

+ https://alabe.com

The Astrology Podcast: A weekly podcast hosted by professional astrologer Chris Brennan.

+ https://theastrologypodcast.com

Magazine

The world's most recognized astrology magazine (available in print and digital formats).

+ https://mountainastrologer.com

Books

+ *Practical Astrology for Witches and Pagans* by Ivo Dominguez, Jr.
+ *Parkers' Astrology: The Definitive Guide to Using Astrology in Every Aspect of Your Life* by Julia and Derek Parker

+ *The Inner Sky: How to Make Wiser Choices for a More Fulfilling Life* by Steven Forrest
+ *Predictive Astrology: Tools to Forecast Your Life and Create Your Brightest Future* by Bernadette Brady
+ *Chart Interpretation Handbook: Guidelines for Understanding the Essentials of the Birth Chart* by Stephen Arroyo
+ *The Art of True Healing: The Unlimited Power of Prayer and Visualization* by Israel Regardie

CONTRIBUTORS

We give thanks and appreciation to all our guest authors who contributed their own special Scorpio energy to this project.

Rhonda Alin

Rhonda is a Psychic and Reader of both Oracle and Tarot cards as well as an instructor and the founder of Northern New Jersey Tarot. She purchased her first deck at age twelve and has studied Tarot with some of the most respected and accomplished readers, authors, and deck designers in the Tarot community. Visit her at www .rhondaalin.com.

Alison Chicosky

Alison Chicosky is a scholar and practitioner of a variety of forms of thaumaturgy with a focus on results-based magic. The founder and force behind Practical Occult (www.practicaloccult.com), she strives to provide enchanted items drawn from a broad background of rigorously studied ancient arts, leveraging the systems of the past for practical modern use.

Cat Heath

Cat is the author of *Elves, Witches, and Gods: Spinning Old Heathen Magic in the Modern Day*. Cat is an animist Heathen and Witch from Lancashire with a passion for obscure texts, magical experimentation (often involving elves), and teaching classes on Heathen magic online. Curious? Follow Cat for more! Blog: http://seohelrune.com.

Dawn Aurora Hunt

Dawn Aurora Hunt, owner of Cucina Aurora Kitchen Witchery, is the author of *A Kitchen Witch's Guide to Love & Romance* and *Kitchen Witchcraft for Beginners*. She combines knowledge of spiritual goals and magickal ingredients to create recipes for all Sun signs in this series. Find her at www .CucinaAurora.com.

Lisa Jade

Jade is an NCGR-PAA1-certified natal astrologer and owner of Living the Liminal, Modern Witchcraft Musings, where she writes and offers readings and birth chart interpretations. Jade is a fourth-degree initiate in the Temple of Witchcraft and lives her life in rural Nova Scotia, Canada, attempting to run a farmstead with integrated permaculture practices.

Sandra Kynes

Sandra Kynes (Midcoast Maine) is the author of seventeen books, including *Mixing Essential Oils for Magic*, *Magical Symbols and Alphabets*, *Crystal Magic*, *Plant Magic*, and *Sea Magic*. Excerpted content from her book *Llewellyn's Complete Book of Correspondences* has been used throughout this series. Find her at http://www.kynes.net.

Wendy Rule

Born on October 31, 1966, Wendy Rule is a world-renowned visionary songstress and Scorpio witch. Originally from Melbourne, Australia, Wendy now lives in a beautiful Victorian home in the New Mexico countryside, where she runs seasonal magical retreats and streams monthly Full Moon Magic concerts on Patreon. Visit her at www.wendyrule.com.

Dayan Skipper-Martinez

Keenly interested in the magic of the past and the paranormal from childhood, Dayan began seriously practicing witchcraft in university. Dayan earned initiation into the Unnamed Path in December of 2016. An animist witch at heart, Dayan seeks out the Mysteries in all their past, present, and future forms.

Notes

Notes

Notes

Notes

Notes